BRILLIANCE

BRILLIANCE

JEWELRY ART
AND
FASHION

EMILY STOEHRER

Contributions by

Bettina Burr, Tanya Crane,
Helen W. Drutt English,
Melanie Grant, Yasmin Hemmerle,
Amin Jaffer, Henrietta Lidchi,
Bella Neyman,
Victoria Reed, Kendall Reiss,
and Joyce J. Scott

MFA PUBLICATIONS
Museum of Fine Arts, Boston

CONTENTS

COLLECTING JEWELRY AT THE MUSEUM OF FINE ARTS, BOSTON

J ewelry's story spans the globe. Picture a sixty-carat emerald mined in South America in the seventeenth century, then carved in India shortly after. The gem is likely set for years in a traditional Indian style—perhaps as a turban ornament—before traveling to the United States in the early twentieth century and becoming the center stone in a brooch fabricated by Oscar Heyman Bros. for Marcus & Co. Around 1929, the piece is purchased by heiress Marjorie Merriweather Post; nearly eighty years later, on June 25, 2008, it is added to the collection of the Museum of Fine Arts, Boston (MFA), where it remains to this day (FIG. 1). The story of just this one brooch stretches across time and space, reflecting artistic movements and global trends, and enriching our understanding of jewelry's place in cultural heritage. How many other stories can the jewelry in the MFA's collection tell?

In the sixteenth century, emeralds like the one featured in Post's brooch were sourced from the New World, in the Viceroyalty of Peru—an area which encompassed present-day Colombia and Ecuador—and traveled to India, where the gems were particular favorites, on Spanish or Portuguese ships.[1] In India, emeralds were valued for their hardness and uniform structure, qualities which made them particularly well suited for carving. The front face of the Post brooch's large central emerald—which features an iris—was probably carved in the seventeenth century, while the back face—on which a daisy appears—seems to reflect a later phase of work, possibly during the eighteenth century.

In the early twentieth century, many Indian gemstones were sold or traded, which created a demand among American, British, and European clientele for carved gems of all sizes. In the late 1920s, the emerald was acquired in Mumbai, then known as Bombay, by William Marcus of Marcus & Co., a prominent American jewelry retailer that rivaled Tiffany & Co. Marcus named it the "Taj Mahal Emerald" for its elaborate carvings of flowers, which he considered similar in style to those that adorn the Indian mausoleum. Upon its arrival in the United States, the emerald was reworked into the bold jewel seen today. It was set in a pendant before being exhibited in 1929, when it served as the centerpiece of an "Indian Arts" tea held in Manhattan.[2] It was soon purchased by Post, and became a favorite jewel of the business executive, philanthropist, and art collector. She wore it as a brooch—a 1952 portrait by Douglas Chandor shows her wearing it on the neckline of her dress. Post wore it in a similar fashion when photographed by Yousuf Karsh just a few years earlier, in 1944 (FIG. 2).

The brooch's acquisition was a defining moment for jewelry at the MFA. It was purchased two years after the 2006 appointment of Yvonne J. Markowitz as the inaugural Rita J. Kaplan and Susan B. Kaplan Curator of Jewelry, an act which made the Museum the first in the United States to champion such a

1 — Oscar Heyman Bros. for Marcus & Co., emerald and diamond brooch, 1929. Platinum, diamond, and emerald.

2 — Yousuf Karsh, portrait of Marjorie Merriweather Post, 1944.

4 — Beads, Nubian, about 1700–1550 BC. Faience.

3 — Bishop's ring, 18th century. Gold, silver, sapphire, and diamond.

position. Markowitz had spent decades working with the MFA's vast collection of Nubian and Egyptian art before shifting into the new role in the David and Roberta Logie Department of Textile and Fashion Arts. With an informal jewelry collection that numbered more than 22,000 objects scattered across nearly every curatorial department, one of the curator's first tasks was to examine pan-Museum holdings to identify areas of strength, explore connections between disparate objects that had never before been in conversation, and craft a plan for the future of jewelry at the MFA.

Although the first pieces of jewelry were added to the collection before the Museum opened its doors to the public in 1876, the Post brooch was a significant strategic acquisition for the institution, as it was the first purchase of fine jewelry made of precious materials. In the more than one hundred years leading up to the gem's accession, jewelry had been added to the collection sporadically, then processed by curators from specialized departments who were not necessarily aware of how those objects fit into the broader narrative of jewelry at the Museum. By contrast, the purchase of the Post brooch demonstrated an institutional commitment to the jewelry collection and an openness to the many stories the field offers. The piece continues to be a vehicle for sharing jewelry's many global stories—it is a gateway to discussions of mining practices; global trade and economics; gem carving; the history of American, Indian, and Islamic art; personal collecting habits; design history; and so much more. As new research is undertaken, the story of this object, and of many others like it, continues to evolve.

This book features a small yet broad sampling of the MFA's extraordinary collection: the oldest object featured was crafted 4,000 years ago in Egypt, while the most recent left the Mumbai workshop of BHAGAT in February 2024 (see fig. 71). The rich history of jewelry at the Museum is punctuated by a series of key moments, beginning in the late nineteenth and early twentieth centuries, when much of the collection—which now totals nearly 25,000 objects—was excavated in Egypt and Sudan, including gold and hardstone amulets such as the *Head of Hathor* (hathor-headed crystal pendant), along with thousands of humble clay beads (fig. 4).

In 1901, the MFA's jewelry holdings further increased when Alice L. Boardman donated nearly three hundred rings to the institution from the collection of her husband, William (fig. 3). The twenty-first century was marked by Susan B. Kaplan's generosity, which helped the Museum build an extraordinary collection of nineteenth-century jewelry, including treasures by Castellani, Carlo Giuliano, Charlotte Newman, and Giacinto Melillo (see figs. 17–18, 143). In 2006, Daphne Farago gifted more than six hundred examples of studio jewelry; her donation of work by American and European artists and makers from the mid-twentieth century until the early years of the twenty-first transformed the collection yet again. In 2018 and 2019, the Toronto-based collector Carole Tanenbaum dramatically added to the MFA's holdings of American costume jewelry and European fashion jewelry. In between these key moments, the Museum has acquired major works, such as Bovin's 1937 starfish brooch, and made great efforts to maintain and expand its collection of contemporary pieces and work by women artists, including Winifred Mason Chenet, Tanya Crane, Elizabeth James Perry, and Asagi Maeda (fig. 5; see figs. 179, 174, 159). Most recently, the addition of work by Anna Hu, BHAGAT, Feng J, Hemmerle, and Wallace Chan has formed a collection of *haute joaillerie*—unique jewels made of precious materials (see figs. 114, 66, 70).

5 — Winifred Mason Chenet, link bracelet, about 1948. Copper and brass.

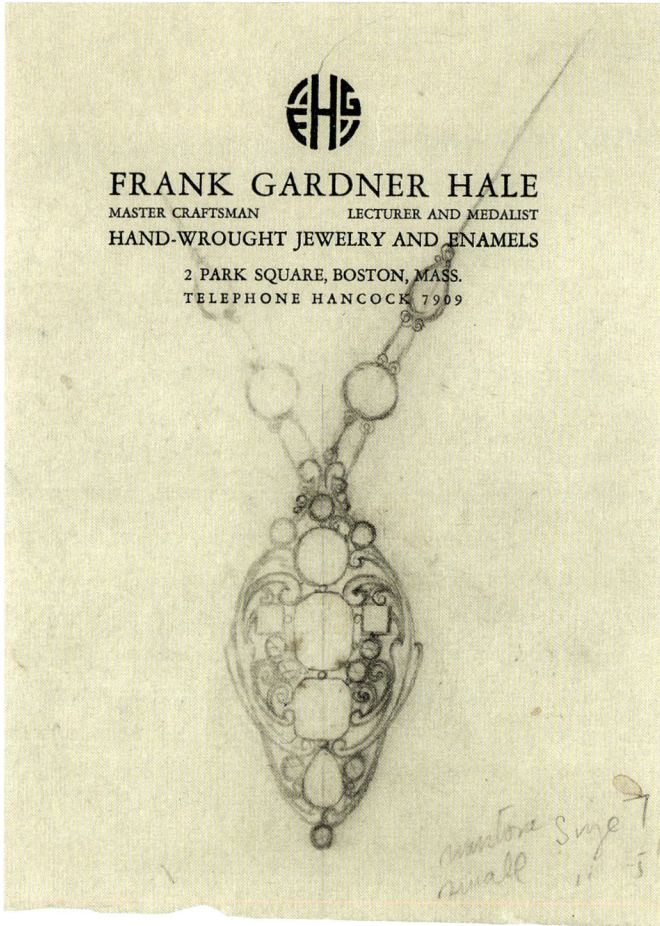

6 — Frank Gardner Hale, design for a necklace, about 1920.

7 — Frank Gardner Hale, jeweled scroll brooch, about 1920. Gold, zircon, diamond, sapphire, and peridot.

The addition of hundreds of books to the Museum library, along with significant numbers of design drawings and documentary materials—such as those of Boston-based Arts and Crafts jeweler Frank Gardner Hale, the New York firm of Trabert & Hoeffer–Mauboussin, and Louis Féron, who fabricated most of Jean Schlumberger's designs for Tiffany & Co.—further established the MFA as a destination for jewelry enthusiasts and scholars to learn more about the field's history, the design process, and technical innovations, as well as study iconic examples of the jeweler's art. Alongside examples of jewelry, these supporting materials aided in the understanding of two important concepts: the field's iterative design process, and the ways designers and fabricators work together (FIGS. 6–7, 177–78).

In 2011, shortly after the creation of the curatorial position, the Rita J. and Stanley H. Kaplan Family Foundation Gallery was unveiled as a space dedicated to the display of jewelry. The introductory exhibition, *Gems, Jewels, and Treasures*, showcased ornaments long part of the MFA's collection, as well as newly acquired works of art and spectacular loans. At the same time, the collection continued to grow and develop. In 2012, the Museum opened the Carol Wall Gallery, a space dedicated to gems and jewelry from the Mediterranean world—objects which had rarely been on view in the museum's 150-year history (FIG. 8). The Kaplan Family Foundation Gallery continued to rotate and evolve over the years, featuring special exhibitions and installations.[3]

On May 18, 2024, with the support of the Nando and Elsa Peretti Foundation, the Rita J. and Stanley H. Family Foundation Gallery reopened after a complete renovation to showcase more than 150 jewels from the collection. Spanning thousands of years of human history, the artifacts in the new permanent exhibition, *Beyond Brilliance,* demonstrate the human desire to adorn the body. The installation—still on display at the time of publication—spotlights many important works of art made since the establishment of the jewelry curatorship, with examples featuring beads, carved shells, diamonds and colored gemstones, precious metals, and more modest materials such as iron, butterfly wings, and human hair. Both *Beyond Brilliance* and this complementary catalogue, *Brilliance,* embrace a thematic approach to the history of jewelry, investigating three universal themes: jewelry as art, as adornment, and as messaging.

8 — Tryphon, Cameo with the wedding of Cupid and Psyche or an initiation rite, Roman, 50–25 BC. Onyx.

MANY
WAYS OF
LOOKING

A piece of jewelry is an object that is worn on the human body, as a decorative and symbolic addition to its outward appearance.
—Marjan Unger [1]

For many thousands of years, jewelry has been created by artists and designers working in a range of styles and materials. An art form and an industry, the field is as multifaceted as the works it encompasses, and includes one-of-a-kind works of art, limited editions, and mass-produced designs. This diversity of artistry covers everything from ancient gems, works rooted in art movements such as Art Deco, studio pieces created by artist-makers or produced in small workshops, costume and fashion jewelry designed to pair with clothing, fine objects crafted of precious materials like gold and diamonds, and contemporary designs made by academically trained artists working in various materials and techniques. Each area boasts a unique history of its own; when considered alongside one another, however, they demonstrate the innovative ways in which humans have adorned their bodies.

Jewelry is an art form so deeply rooted in humanity that it connects with and communicates to people across age, culture, and gender. From something made by one's child to a treasured family heirloom, a cherished wedding ring or a sentimental gem given or received as a gift, jewelry allows us to hold personal memories close, bringing great joy or even sorrow. As artist and educator Bruce Metcalf argued in his seminal essay "On the Nature of Jewelry" (1993), while conversations on jewelry typically stress design, craftsmanship, and use, it is through its "social and psychological utility" that jewelry holds "the ability to touch people."[2] Metcalf outlined five functions of the art form: it serves as a point of connection with the body, as personal decoration, as a method of communicating social messages, as portable wealth, and in mediation with the spiritual. More recently, Dutch scholar and collector Marjan Unger elaborated on the role of jewelry in society, stressing the human body's link to jewelry—a seemingly obvious, but often overlooked, component of study.[3] Her writing offers a big-picture view of universal themes in the field, and examines jewelry's position as both a vehicle for memory and a key element of fashion.[4]

Jewelry indeed functions in numerous ways, public and private. It comes to life on the body, where it is simultaneously a decorative art, an object of adornment, and a silent messenger. Examined as a decorative art, jewelry relates to broader artistic movements, embraces new materials, and incorporates—or begets—technical innovations. When worn as an element of dress, jewelry expresses ideas of beauty and sartorial style. Displayed on the body, jewelry can express personal beliefs and attitudes. These three functions of jewelry intertwine, moving nimbly throughout history and across cultures—and even sometimes shifting meaning.

JEWELRY IS AN ART. Surviving from antiquity, jewelry offers a physical trace of human life. One such example from the MFA's collection is a detailed gold figure of Nike, goddess of victory, from the Late Classical or Early Hellenistic period. Soldered together from more than one hundred individual elements and modeled in the round, this ancient adornment remains a tour-de-force example of the goldsmith's art, and possesses a sense of dynamism that exceeds its small size (FIG. 9). Nike—who wears a belted tunic known as a chiton, a full-length dress, and several items of jewelry—leans forward, her left hand pulling on the reins of two horses. The goddess's posture is confident, while the horses raise their two front hooves as if startled. A small hoop on the underside was probably attached to an ear wire, indicating the jewel was once an earring, perhaps worn by royalty or decorating a statue.

Created thousands of years later, artist Mary Lee Hu's *Choker #88* offers a contemporary illustration of the jeweler's—and goldsmith's—art. Hu, who studied at the prestigious Cranbrook Academy of Art, has spent much of her career creating gold jewelry using methods borrowed from basketry and textile weaving. She developed this technique in 1976, during an attempt to replicate the surface texture of a Native American Northwest Coast cedar bark basket. The resulting method, which Hu calls double twining, became a signature of the artist, who has been using the technique almost exclusively in the nearly fifty years since. In the complex *Choker #88*—one of Hu's largest ornaments—she employed double twining to create a fluid and dynamic line, crafting a sculpture that encircles the neck (FIG. 10). Borrowing techniques from adjacent traditions, Hu's work offers the field of jewelry an approach unlike what's come before, yet, in doing so, joins a long tradition of technical mastery and innovation in jewelry design. As with Hu's other works, *Choker #88* is sensitive to issues of scale and weight, complete only when resting upon the wearer's shoulders.

JEWELRY ADORNS. It comes to life on the body, and acts as an extension of fashion trends as well as one's personal style. Over time, buttons, fasteners, and ornaments evolved beyond the merely functional to become beautiful luxury objects and fashion statements in their own right. At the same time, the rise of mass production in the late nineteenth and twentieth centuries led artists and designers to quickly make both inexpensive and more costly ornaments to complement clothing styles. American costume jewelers like Miriam Haskell responded to demand with designs that were as creative and technically innovative as fine jewelry. Haskell, under the creative direction of Frank Hess, became known for producing high-quality, handmade jewelry using

IO — Mary Lee Hu, *Choker #88*, 2005. Gold.

European materials. Her extravagant jewels brightened ensembles during the Great Depression and World War II, when women who could afford precious jewelry didn't want to flaunt it, and during the booming postwar years, when oversized "cocktail" and fun novelty jewels grew in popularity. By 1933, Haskell occupied three floors of a Fifth Avenue building in New York City, and in 1936, she opened a boutique in Saks Fifth Avenue. She presented five collections annually; each included accessories to be worn with evening, afternoon, and daywear. Her collectors included Joan Crawford and Lucille Ball, who wore the jeweler's works on television. One wood and glass bead "necklace" Haskell designed in the 1940s allowed the wearer an element of creativity—it lacks a clasp to secure it around the neck (FIG. II). Instead, clips on the back of the jewel's wooden flowers allow it to attach to the neckline of a blouse or dress, worn slightly differently each time.

II — Miriam Haskell Company,
wood sautoir, 1940–49. Brass, wood,
glass, and silk.

12 — Art Smith, *Ellington*, about 1958.
Silver, turquoise, rhodonite, chalcedony,
and amazonite.

13 — Wesekh broad collar, Egyptian, 2246–2152 BC. Gold, steatite, turquoise, and lapis lazuli.

Created shortly thereafter, and on a smaller scale, Afro-Cuban artist Art Smith's 1958 *Ellington* necklace also makes a sartorial statement, demanding simplicity from any ensemble it graces. Smith was part of a network of mid-century makers known as the Studio Jewelers, so named because they designed and produced one-of-a-kind works of art, often made and sold in their own galleries and shops (FIG. 12). Like many of his peers, Smith worked in New York City's Greenwich Village, where he was immersed in the burgeoning art scene. His retail space and studio pulsed with the rhythms of jazz music and was a popular hang out for his famous friends and clients, such as renowned choreographer Talley Beatty. *Ellington*, named for jazz legend Duke Ellington, includes many of the basic tenets of Smith's work: a sense of movement with its rhythmic line, bold size, and open areas through which the body—or a garment—may be glimpsed, becoming part of the design.[5] The close connections among the body, clothing, and jewelry existed well before the twentieth century and continue today. As part of one's sartorial choices, the body is a blank canvas where jewelry plays a key role in creating a fashionable look or defining an individual's style.

JEWELRY SENDS A MESSAGE. Jewelry can communicate across a room, or across time. Is the wearer engaged? Mourning? Making a political statement? Demonstrating power, or their position? Jewelry can tell a story, send a message, or speak to one's position within a group. Take the broad collar of Ptahshepses Impy, an Egyptian official of King Pepy II, for example (FIG. 13). Indicating rank and status, the necklace communicates into the great beyond. While it boasts two gold terminals upon which Ptahshepses's name is inscribed, the majority of the necklace is constructed of stone beads strung on cord—one of the earliest jewelry-making techniques. The broad collar's striking turquoise and lapis lazuli, rare materials, likely made their way from mines in the Sinai Peninsula and Afghanistan to Egypt and Nubia, where expert craftspeople carved them into beads.

Materials, however, do not need to be rare in order to speak loudly. The visionary artist Joyce J. Scott realizes the possibility that the humble bead offers, using the medium to confront challenging subjects such as racism and sexism. Her glass bead necklace *Adam and Eve*—made sculptural through Scott's expert use of the peyote stitch, an improvisational weaving technique—urges viewers to consider the biblical creation story (FIGS. 14–15). The necklace "depicts Eve at the moment she tastes the forbidden fruit, tangled in vines and grotesque faces…challenging the viewer to consider the burden of gender stereotypes born from Eve's temptation."[6] Scott's work transforms beads into jewelry that invites uncomfortable conversations about humanity's past and present.

14–15 — Joyce J. Scott, *Adam and Eve*, 1985. Glass, wire, and nylon.

As you read this catalogue, consider how these three functions of jewelry speak to one another. Ponder the many hands involved in the making of each object, from the creativity of the designer to the technical mastery of the craftsperson; the skill of the lapidary who cut the gemstone to the lifestyles of the people who purchased, inherited, or were given these objects. Imagine how these jewels were worn, and consider the meanings they have held. Listen to the varied voices throughout, including the scholarship and reflections of ten artists, curators, and collectors, who offer new insights and fresh perspectives on these objects.

An essential art form, jewelry both reflects the styles of the day and serves as a vehicle for artistic expression. Each piece a work of art in its own right, the jewelry showcased in this chapter demonstrates its makers' extraordinary craftsmanship and mastery of materials, including glass, gold, enamel, and even plastic. Some works were designed and fabricated by a single jeweler; others were created by individuals who worked across media—photographers, sculptors, architects. What these objects have in common, however, is their connection to global art movements: when these pieces were made, they expressed new ideas about art and culture that reflected, responded to, and engaged with larger artistic conversations. Throughout time, as artists have made—and continue to make—jewelry, whether traditional, vanguard, or both, many have paid homage to historical styles, connected with larger contemporary trends, or pushed boundaries to embrace new materials and techniques.

Nineteenth-century Western artists in particular were deeply inspired by history. As many jewelers looked to past cultures for inspiration, a series of revival styles emerged, including archeological, Classical, Egyptian, Gothic, and Renaissance. Some copied directly from previous works, while others combined elements from various eras to form a pastiche of historical styles. The opening of European and American museums as well as the formation of publications like architect Owen Jones's seminal sourcebook, *The Grammar of Ornament*, in 1856, which illustrated global design styles, fueled creative imaginations around the world.

Among the most celebrated jewelers working in the archeological revival style was the Castellani family in Rome—a standout maker even in a city that boasted 1,500 goldsmiths. Founded by Fortunato Pio Castellani in 1814, the family's eponymous jewelry house began as a retailer, and their shop—eventually located across from the Trevi Fountain—became known for their collection of exquisite imported styles from Parisian firms like Mellerio. Castellani's priorities began to shift in 1836, when the papal government invited Fortunato and his thirteen-year-old son, Alessandro, to examine and restore gold ornaments excavated from Etruscan tombs in Cerveteri, Italy. Young Alessandro was particularly fascinated by the granulation he saw on several pieces, the ancient decorative technique of embellishing gold sheets with minute spheres a goldsmith's dream. After years of experimentation, he mastered the art, and joined the family firm alongside his brother Augusto. By the 1850s, Castellani had become unmatched in technical prowess, combining their skill in creating jewelry inspired by ancient Etruscan metalsmiths with a contemporary style which incorporated historical iconography. Their jewelry was a political and fashion statement that marked its wearers as intellectuals as well as connoisseurs of the fine arts.[2]

As the firm's specialties grew to include granulation as well as micromosaic, Castellani's aesthetic shifted toward ancient styles in an attempt to "re-create what they saw as Italy's national heritage."[3] Their participation in international expositions helped to establish a trend of archeological-style jewelry, and eventually the firm expanded, establishing locations in Paris and Naples. In Rome, the family's shop sold ancient treasures sourced from excavations in Tuscany in addition to designs from their own workshops. Castellani's success coincided with a wave of Italian nationalism, and the firm, along with fellow jewelers, sought to evoke what they saw as the glorious past in ornaments with artistic— and political—meanings. Their devotion to Italian unification led the jeweler to declare a "war on fashion" by 1851, ceasing sales of imported works to focus on creating their own designs celebrating Italian history.[4] The family's nationalist beliefs were so strong that Alessandro was exiled from Rome for ten years, beginning in the 1860s, for participating in an 1859 rebellion.[5]

Castellani also helped to assemble major collections of ancient jewelry, and likely guided Giovanni Pietro Campana, director of the Sacro Monte di Pietà, in amassing a major private collection of Etruscan goldsmithing. When Campana was arrested in 1859 for embezzling from the Vatican to fund this endeavor, the Sacro Monte's jewelry was left with Castellani for repair and sale. The family asserted that they could not imagine Campana's collection leaving the country, as they viewed it as an indispensable piece of Italian history. Nevertheless, in 1860, just one year after taking responsibility for the jewels, they sold the collection to Napoleon III of France. Before the jewelry traveled from Rome to Paris, however, the company cast and later copied examples from Campana's collection, seeking to capture and sustain a piece of Italy's history. One such brooch, now housed at the MFA Boston, is a copy Castellani made of an item from the Sacro Monte: a pair of gold earrings with a quatrefoil design and granulation that today is part of the Louvre's collection of ancient jewelry (FIGS. 16–17) The reproduction is an extraordinary example of the way history directly influenced Castellani's style, and a prime specimen of the jeweler's skill in granulation.

Unlike granulation, micromosaic jewelry has no precedent in antiquity, yet Castellani worked in both techniques when creating their archeological revival–style pieces. They drew on the findings of eighteenth- and nineteenth-century excavations, which unearthed floor mosaics, works of art where small tesserae—bits of stone, tile, glass, and other materials—were pieced together to form a coherent picture. Castellani's jewelry miniaturized that technique. One such tiny treasure is a brooch likely made by Luigi Podi, who headed the firm's micromosaic workshop from 1851 until 1888 (FIG. 18).[6] The piece, which features a circular micromosaic panel with the head of a lion against a cream ground, echoes Roman floor mosaics while demonstrating the exceptional skill

16 (OPPOSITE, TOP) — Disc-shaped earrings, Etruscan, 550–500 BC. Gold.

17 (OPPOSITE, BOTTOM) — Castellani, brooch, about 1859. Gold.

18 (RIGHT) — Castellani, lion brooch, about 1870. Gold and glass.

and ingenuity of Castellani's craftsmen, many of whom were trained in Vatican workshops. The inspiration for the design, made up of thousands of meticulously placed small glass tesserae, likely came from a mosaic of a lion found in the House of Centaur in Pompeii in 1829, about forty years before the brooch was created. In reducing the scale of these works to create a piece of wearable art, Castellani's workshop created a painterly work that is connected to Italian history, yet unique to the nineteenth century.

Castellani were not alone in looking to the past for inspiration. Indeed, historical techniques such as granulation continued to seduce makers such as John Paul Miller well into the twentieth century. The jeweler's 1995 *Polyp Colony* necklace features Miller's unique style of enameling and showcases his highly sophisticated goldsmithing (FIG. 20). The pendant and hand-wrought loop-in-loop chain recall the work of ancient artisans whom Miller and Castellani alike admired; Miller was particularly influenced by the metalwork of the ancient Etruscans, especially their use of gold granulation.

Jewelry artists continue to push the boundaries of what's possible. Beginning in the 1990s, Italian artist Giovanni Corvaja's interest in the Golden Fleece of Greek myth led him to experiment with the ductility of metal wire in hopes of creating a form of gold fine and soft enough to mimic sheep's wool.

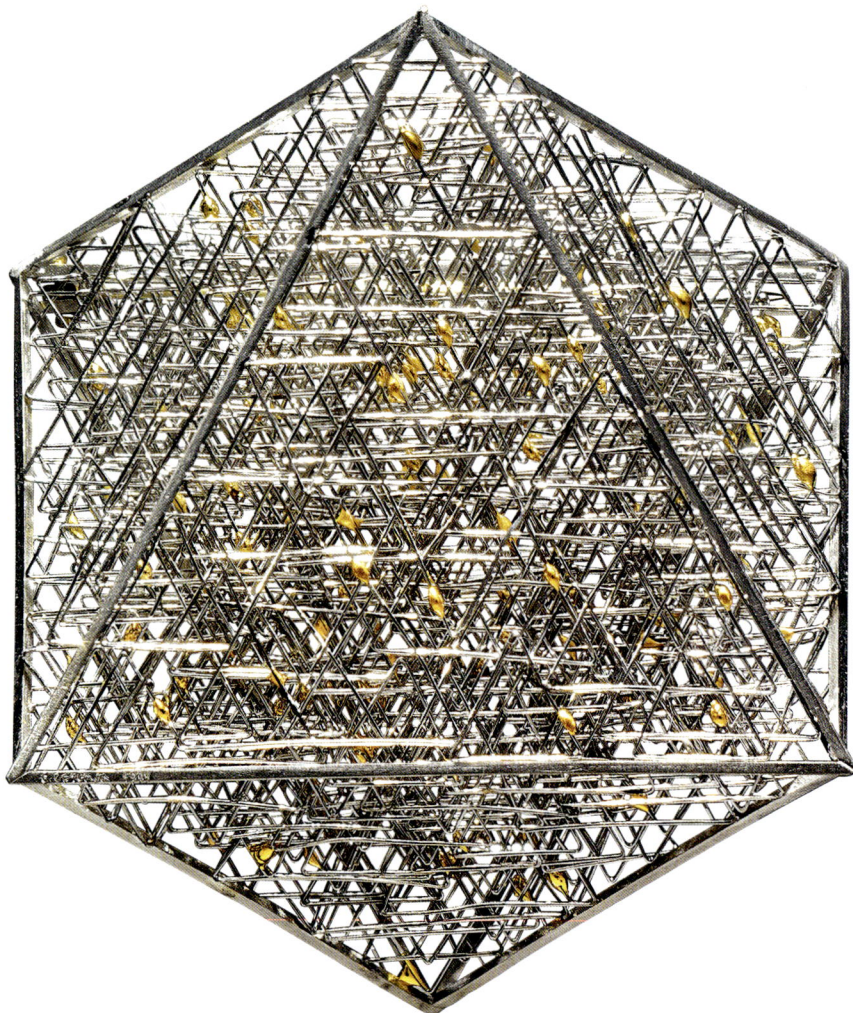

20 — Giovanni Corvaja, *Spille*, 1999. Platinum and gold.

19 (OPPOSITE) — John Paul Miller, *Polyp Colony*, 1995. Gold and enamel.

Corvaja's 1999 *Spille* brooch reflects these early days of experimentation: the artist worked with gold and platinum to create a geometric frame crossed with thin wires, then masterfully added granulation to the metal surfaces (FIG. 19). Over the next decade, he continued to draw wires thinner and thinner, even developing a three-dimensional knitting technique that allowed him to build strong forms using flexible metal threads. This work culminated in 2008 and 2009, when Corvaja unveiled his *Golden Fleece Ring* and *Golden Fleece Headpiece*, respectively.[7] The latter is a wearable accessory, entirely made of gold, that mimics the look and feel of a fur-trimmed hat.

In the American Southwest, three contemporary jewelers are also looking to the past in order to forge forward, learning and expanding upon techniques pioneered by previous artists. In the 1970s, Indigenous artist Angie Reano Owen revived an ancient stone-on-shell inlay technique previously practiced

21—22 — Charlene Sanchez Reano and Frank Reano, *Thunderbird*, 2009. Turquoise, spiny oyster shell, jet, mother-of-pearl, lapis lazuli, and melon shell.

by her Pueblo ancestors. The once-lost art form involves laying a mosaic of small rectangular stones in a herringbone design and setting it in shell. Although Pueblo communities of the American Southwest were—and remain—well known for their lapidary work, which involves the cutting and polishing of precious materials like gemstones and shell, the inlay technique was largely forgotten until Owen learned, reviving the craft (SEE FIGS. 68—69). After mastering stone-on-shell inlay to create designs deeply rooted in her culture's rich past, Owen taught it to family members, some of whom were well-known heishi, or shell, beadmakers. Her brother, Frank Reano, and his wife, Charlene, used the technique to create their *Thunderbird* necklace, a reversible piece with forty-nine inlaid tabs offering a different combination of colors on each side. One side of the necklace, which represents a stylized thunderbird,

features blue turquoise, dark orange spiny oyster shell, black jet, and white, black, and gold mother-of-pearl (FIG. 21). The reverse is dominated by blue turquoise throughout, with a ring of deep orange spiny oyster shell in the center and highlights of dark blue lapis, creamy melon shell, and shiny white mother-of-pearl (FIG. 22). *Thunderbird*, like much of the work of the Owen and Reano families, reveals the makers' place not only in the strong tradition of lapidary artists from Santo Domingo Pueblo, but also as part of the revival of the stone-on-shell technique, which had been considered lost to history. By combining these traditional Pueblo skills with the tribal iconography of the thunderbird, Owen and the Reanos make the past a vital part of their contemporary art practice and connect their work to a broader tradition of reviving the art of one's predecessors.

23 — Jaguar effigy pendant, Diquís, 700–1520. Gold-copper alloy.

Jewelry artists borrow not just techniques from earlier periods, but iconography as well, embracing historical forms and meanings. One such example is the New York–born artist William Spratling, who played a key role in the twentieth-century revival of Mexican silversmithing. In the late 1920s, Spratling visited the village of Taxco outside of Mexico City, known for its silver mines. After repeat trips to the area, Spratling settled there in 1929, and, in 1931, he founded El Taller de las Delicias (Studio of Delights), a workshop where he designed and made silver jewelry. Much of his work looked to ancient Mesoamerican iconography and Indigenous art forms. Images of felines, especially the jaguar, appeared in the artwork of nearly all major Mesoamerican cultures, representing power and strength. One ancient pendant in the MFA's collection features the same subject as a brooch by Spratling: a jaguar whose rounded front claws cleverly double as rings through which a cord could be threaded (FIG. 23). Spratling's brooch elongated the feline form, making it appear as if the large cat is leaping (FIG. 24).

24 — William Spratling, jaguar brooch, 1940–46. Silver and amethyst.

Periods of historical reference are sometimes met with an avant-garde response by those looking to break with the past and create something markedly different. In the years leading up to the twentieth century—after decades of historical revivals—jewelry artists were especially taken with Art Nouveau, which offered an aesthetic unlike anything seen before. The movement attracted attention in 1900 at the Exposition Universelle (World Fair) in Paris, when René Lalique and others first presented Art Nouveau jewelry to an international audience. Their pieces and those that followed—primarily made in France and Belgium—were beautiful in design and execution, yet often haunting in subject matter. Characterized by sinuous lines, sensuous female figures, and subjects such as flowers, insects, and natural forms, Art Nouveau jewelry was at once captivating and repulsive.

The allure of the female figure was one of the style's more popular themes, and women were often depicted as nude and highly feminized, with swirling hair and subdued expressions. One piece shown at the 1900 exposition,

25 — Henri Vever and Eugène Samuel Grasset, *Apparitions*, about 1899. Gold and enamel.

designed by graphic artist Eugène Samuel Grasset and made by jeweler Henri Vever, juxtaposes feminine allure with horror. Titled *Apparitions*, the brooch depicts two heads—one masculine and one feminine—emerging from a watery surface (FIG. 25). A ghostly head in the foreground, illustrated with long golden tresses, rises from the swirling water, a horrified dark-haired man lurking behind.

Grasset and Vever's brooch also demonstrates Art Nouveau's fascination with Japanese culture. The imagery in *Apparitions* recalls a Japanese ghost story about a beautiful woman who lures young men to a watery grave, and the female figure's face is similar to the *ko-omote* masks worn in Noh theater, while the stylized water is evocative of *karakusa* patterns. Vever and Grasset were not alone in their admiration of these designs; the jewelers were among a group of early twentieth-century artists enamored with the arts of Japan. Demonstrating a similar haunting beauty, contemporary Japanese artist Shinji Nakaba reversed this stream of cross-cultural influence, looking at European art to create his *Peace* brooch (FIG. 26). The large oval brooch captures a face that looks as if it's pushing through stone, like a death mask or a spirit coming through a wall. Nakaba carved the figure from a helmet, or cameo, shell, once home to an enormous sea snail. The shell's large peaks provided the artist with great depth and material for sculpting. Looking at Greek art and thinking about historical antecedents, the artist intentionally carved an ambiguous figure. A brownish-orange streak, a natural color change within the shell, runs down the person's face. Are they crying? Dead? Asleep? Like Grasset and Vever's *Apparitions*, the *Peace* brooch is narrative, but its story is unspoken. The jewel leaves the viewer to draw their own conclusions.

27 — Louis Comfort Tiffany for Tiffany & Co., necklace, about 1910. Opal, demantoid garnet, sapphire, and gold. Left to right: front and back.

American jewelry artists of the late nineteenth and early twentieth centuries responded to the Arts and Crafts movement with similar excitement as Grasset and Vever did to Art Nouveau, even becoming emblems of the style. Louis Comfort Tiffany, who headed Tiffany Studios and later Tiffany & Co., was one of the great masters of American Arts and Crafts. Using the resources of the jewelry house founded by his father, Charles Lewis Tiffany, in tandem with his own less commercial and more artistic aesthetic, Comfort Tiffany combined gemstones and metal in fresh and exciting ways. Like the work of many of his peers in the Arts and Crafts style, his jewelry features an intensive interest in nature, and while his stained-glass windows, lamps, and metalwork include familiar motifs of dragonflies, fish, and flowers, in Comfort Tiffany's designs, nature surrounds rare or important gemstones. Working closely with the company's gemologist, George Frederick Kunz, the jeweler created garland frames to highlight exceptional gemstones like this black opal, a particularly large and spectacular example of a stone only discovered in 1877

(FIG. 27). Suspended from a gold chain, the opal is ensconced in a meandering gold vine on the front and back; the open back reveals the matrix rock in which the gem was found.

A contemporary of Louis Comfort Tiffany, G. Paulding Farnham worked at Tiffany & Co. from 1885 to 1908, eventually serving as the company's chief designer and director of jewelry. During his time there, Farnham's designs utilized the rainbow of gems sourced by Kunz. The designer, who went on to be known for his eclectic influences, was particularly celebrated for his orchid brooches, exhibited at the 1889 Paris exposition.[8] One such ornament, worn on the back of the hand and held in place by four finger rings and a bracelet, was designed after an Indian *hathpal*, meaning flower for the hand (FIG. 28).

28 — G. Paulding Farnham for Tiffany & Co., hand ornament, about 1893. Gold, turquoise, sapphire, garnet, zircon, peridot, beryl, tourmaline, chrysoberyl, and pearl.

29 — Josephine Hartwell Shaw, necklace, 1910–18. Gold, jade, and glass.

30 — Marie Zimmermann, bangles, late 1930s. Gold, jade, carnelian, and enamel.

Farnham had studied with Edward C. Moore, who held one of the United States' largest collections of Islamic and Hindu art in the late nineteenth century.[9] Moore trained Farnham to look both directly at nature and at objects in museum collections and libraries for inspiration.

Farnham and Louis Comfort Tiffany's early twentieth-century contemporaries Josephine Hartwell Shaw and Marie Zimmermann were equally fascinated by historical materials and precedents. Shaw and Zimmermann both incorporated broken, or "found," pieces of Chinese jade in their jewelry. An early member of Boston's Society of Arts and Crafts, Shaw designed and fabricated her own creations, including a gold, jade, and glass necklace made on private commission for Mrs. Atherton Loring of Boston. In a 1915 *House Beautiful* article, Shaw described how the stone "suggests the setting," an idea evident in the central elements of the necklace: two pieces of pale green Chinese jade, complemented by green-toned gold and polished rectangular plaques of green glass (FIG. 29).[10] A sophisticated composition and Shaw's most important surviving jewel, the necklace boasts a harmonious interplay of forms, colors, and contrasting textures. Working in Boston and later in Duxbury, Massachusetts, the artist created works that were highly acclaimed beyond her home state, exhibiting her jewelry at the Cleveland Decorative Arts Club in 1908 and the Art Institute of Chicago in 1911 and 1918.

Shaw's contemporary, Marie Zimmermann, was educated at the Art Students League and the Pratt Institute. Her choices of material varied widely, and her design interests ranged from Egyptian and Classical to Chinese art. In the late 1930s, Zimmermann created a pair of bangles using Chinese jade

31 — D'Ora, Madame Jean Lassalle wearing jewelry by Jean Fouquet and a hat by Madame Agnès, 1929.

32 — Art Deco brooch, United States, about 1925–30. Silver, lapis lazuli, and onyx.

sourced from a broken "dragon playing pearl"–style bangle, combined with a polychrome enameled dragon head set atop a green-scaled body. The bangles were shown in an exhibition of the artist's work in Santa Barbara, California, in 1939, and they remained in her possession for the rest of her life (FIG. 30).

By the time Zimmermann exhibited these bracelets, popular fashions had shifted from the Arts and Crafts movement's emphasis on design and craftsmanship and rejection of industrialization toward the more geometric styles of the 1920s, followed by the streamlined Modernism of the 1930s. In 1929, Jean Fouquet, Raymond Templier, and Gérard Sandoz, three of France's leading jewelers, abruptly left the Société des Artistes Décorateurs—a professional organization made up of decorative artists and designers of furniture and interiors—to become part of a new avant-garde group known as the Union des Artistes Modernes (UAM). Members of the UAM sought to create art that was free of ornamentation and unlike anything that had come before. Jean Fouquet, son of renowned Art Nouveau jeweler Georges Fouquet, rejected his father's sweeping, tendril-like designs to create works that embraced geometry, found inspiration in industry, and favored a Cubist aesthetic. One brooch in the MFA's collection, though not made by the artist, strongly resembles a Fouquet brooch worn by Madame Jean Lassalle in a photograph taken by D'Ora (Dora Kallmus) for the French fashion magazine *L'Officiel de la couture et de mode de Paris* in

33 — Auguste Bonaz, Machine
Age necklace, 1930–37. Chrome and
plastic (Galalith).

35 — Pablo Picasso, *Girl Before a Mirror*, 1932.

34 — Wendy Ramshaw, *Girl Before a Mirror*, 1989. Rings: silver and resin; stand: nickel alloy and resin.

March 1929 (The official [publication] of Paris couture and fashion; FIGS. 31–32). Such an imitation was not unique; pieces by UAM members were copied by jewelers such as Jakob Bengel in Idar-Oberstein, Germany, as well as by others working in Europe and the United States.

The French house of Auguste Bonaz incorporated not just industrial inspirations, but industrial materials, in their work, pioneering the use of synthetics in jewelry design (FIG. 33). Likely influenced by his father's work manufacturing hair combs and related accessories, Bonaz experimented with Galalith, a plastic derived from the milk protein casein. After his death in 1922, the house was made famous by Bonaz's wife, Marguerite, who expanded the firm's wares. The jewelry created under her direction embraced the period's Art Deco movement, echoing the more costly jewelry offered by UAM members.

The strong geometry of Art Deco and Cubist jewelry extended far beyond the movements' heydays, including the years post–World War II. Of note is the work of British artist Wendy Ramshaw, who studied illustration and design before pursuing jewelry. Her earliest works, pieces of paper jewelry, were sold at Bazaar, a London boutique owned by fashion designer Mary Quant. After this early success, Ramshaw attended Central Saint Martin's School of Art and Design, where she began to make one-of-a-kind objects, including the ring stacks for which she became well known. Each of these is a unique sculpture intended to display rings when not in use (FIG. 34). The MFA's ring stack, *Girl Before a Mirror*, draws on a 1932 Picasso painting of the same title, the black and silver stripes of Ramshaw's stand and nine rings echoing the stylized garment worn by the Spanish artist's figure (FIG. 35). Working more than fifty years after Picasso, Ramshaw abstracted the titular girl's form, offering collectors a way to step into the mirror, select and don a ring, and thus embody the art.

The concept of stepping through the looking glass connects to the Surrealist art of the 1930s, which offered a bizarre lens through which to view the world. Working after the European peak of the movement, the Greenwich Village artists Carol and Sam Kramer collaborated to create the Surrealist *Lovers* brooch. Sam Kramer, an eccentric in the same vein as outlandish artist Salvador Dalí, billed himself as the maker of "Fantastic Jewelry for People Who are Slightly Mad," and maintained a Greenwich Village shop and studio that became a gathering place for local artists.[11] The jeweler's Surrealist sensibilities were evident in the design of the studio itself: to enter the shop, visitors had to reach out and caress the doorknob, a human hand that Kramer dressed in a glove during the winter. Kramer collaborated with his wife, Carol, also a talented jeweler, to create the *Lovers* brooch (FIG. 36). The artists fabricated the gem in three metal planes, each riveted and hinged so that the two lovers can be manipulated, moved apart, and brought back together. Bezel-set cabochon

37 — Noma Copley, pencil bracelet, 1999. Gold, coral, wood, and steel.

stones, strategically placed on the male figure, add color and dimension to the dynamic, erotic ornament, which writer Mark Foley described as "a battle of the sexes…a Rorschach Test in metal—deliberately ambiguous, multivocal, and provocative."[12] The abstracted bodies in *Lovers* are not unlike the abstracted figures of Dalí.

Surrealism's impact on jewelry was felt through the end of the twentieth century, as artists such as Noma Copley continued to distort reality in their creations. An American who expatriated to Paris after World War II, Copley befriended and collected the work of many Surrealist artists during her time in France. In 1967, at age fifty, Copley began making jewelry, and her designs—especially those from the late twentieth century—reflect her close connection to the movement. One such piece, made in 1999, transforms an everyday object—the number two pencil—into wearable sculpture. Here, Copley elevates the ubiquitous yellow writing instrument into a gold bangle with a red coral eraser at one end and a steel point at the other (FIG. 37).

Around the time Copley started her career as a jeweler, her friend Man Ray, a key member of the Dada and Surrealist groups in early twentieth-century Paris, also ventured into the field. Commissioned by GianCarlo Montebello and Teresa Pomodoro, fabricators who asked some of the twentieth century's most notable artists to apply their skills to jewelry, Man Ray adapted a lampshade he designed in 1919 into a pair of oversized curled earrings titled *Pendants*

38 — Man Ray, *Catherine Deneuve*, 1968.

39 — Man Ray for GEM Montebello, *Pendants Pending*, 1970. Gold.

Pending (FIG. 39).[13] The dramatic shoulder-dusting earrings, made in the GEM Montebello workshop in Milan, belong to an edition of twelve, which was produced alongside a smaller version of the pendants called *Les Boucles* (Curls). French actress Catherine Deneuve famously wore a pair of the larger earrings in a photograph taken by Man Ray in 1968 (FIG. 38). Unlike traditional earrings that are pushed through the ear or clipped to the lobe, *Pendants Pending* hang from a wire that sits over the back of the ear.

In addition to their collaboration with Man Ray, GEM Montebello partnered with many artists famous from working in other media to translate their designs to jewelry. In some ways, this approach was modeled after the work of multimedia artist Alexander Calder, whose handmade jewelry met widespread acclaim starting in the 1940s and inspired mid-century studio jewelers such as Art Smith. A pair of Calder's kinetic earrings, made of hammered silver wire, move with the body like the artist's mobiles do in the air (FIG. 40). Though he primarily gifted his jewelry to friends and family, such as painter Georgia O'Keeffe, Calder's pieces were also sold at Joan Sonnabend's revolutionary Sculpture to Wear gallery in Manhattan's Plaza Hotel.

More recently, Iraqi British architect Zaha Hadid designed a collection for the Danish jewelry house Georg Jensen. Hadid, who was known as the "Queen of the Curve," incorporated the ingenuity of her architectural forms into her eight-piece collection, fabricated in silver using Jensen's sleek, Modernist style. Jensen's managing director, Meeling Wong, described "the curvilinear forms, organic silhouettes and sweeping lines that make up Hadid's architectural DNA" as "ingrained within the collection," the "defining piece" of which—according to Hadid herself—was the *Lamellae Twisted Cuff* (FIGS. 41–42).[14] The bracelet's title is the plural of *lamella*, a word meaning thin layers. Hadid's twisted, textured cuff miniaturizes her monumental building designs, such as the Heydar Aliyev Cultural Centre in Azerbaijan, allowing fans of the architect to embody her ideas (FIG. 43). Worn close to the body, the cuff—like all the other jewelry described on these pages—allows collectors to adorn their body with decorative art as a reminder of what they find beautiful or wondrous.

Jewelry *is* art—artists and designers who create jewelry make pieces of wearable sculpture. Sometimes design and craftsmanship bring the art form

40 — Alexander Calder, earrings, 1940–45. Silver.

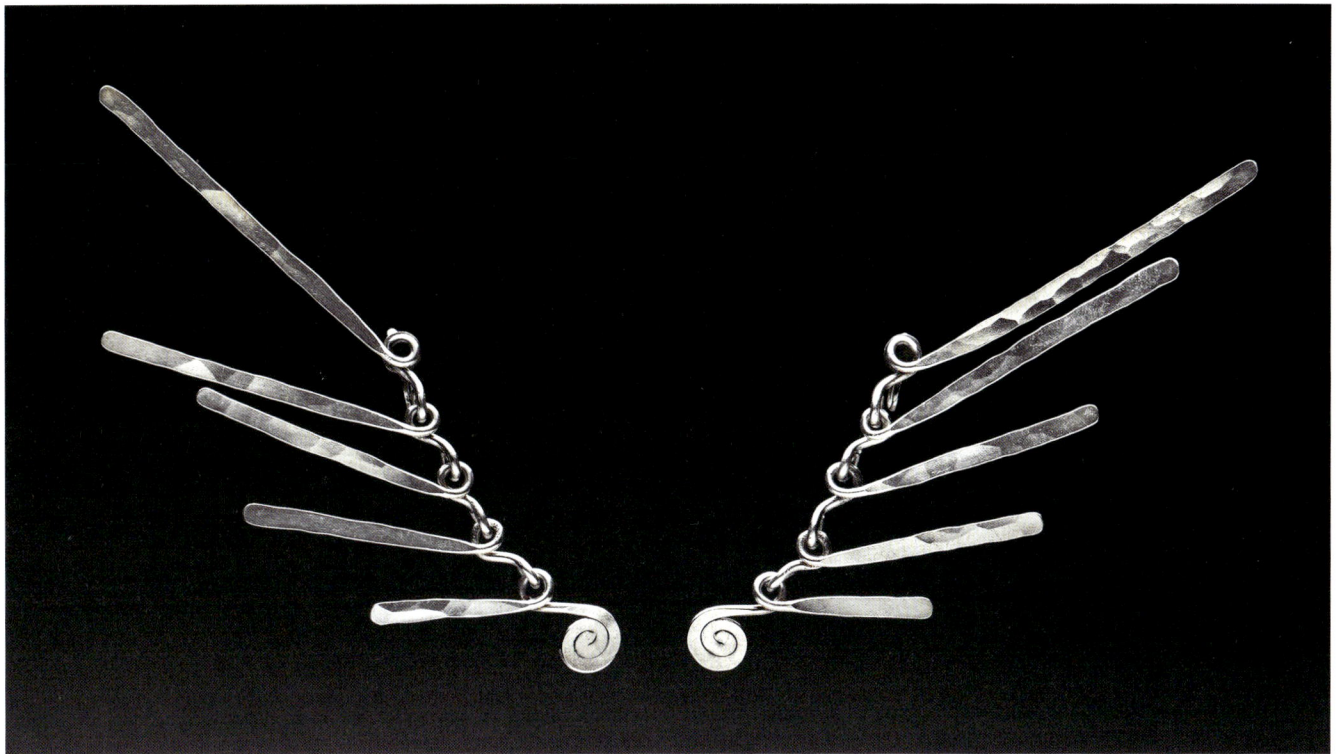

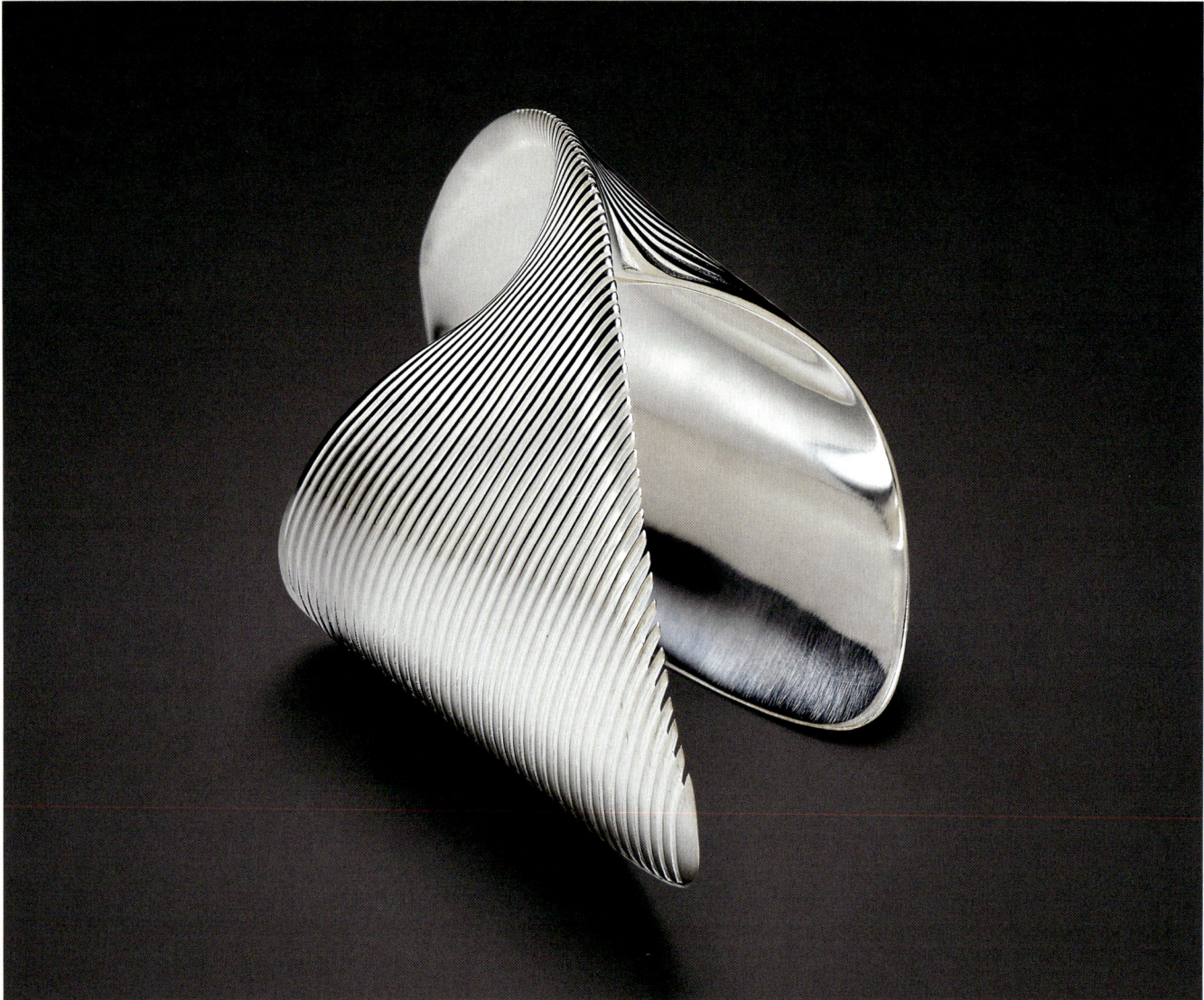

41 — Zaha Hadid for Georg Jensen, *Lamellae Twisted Cuff*, 2016. Silver.

into close contact with the zeitgeist. At other times, it exists on the edges, with jewelers working in traditional manners using tried and tested materials and techniques; still others push boundaries, pioneering new methods. Over the last seventy-five years, jewelry artists have worked within larger art movements while innovating new approaches, introducing found objects, or creating luxury markets for industrial metals such as titanium. Just as techniques like goldsmithing have historically been learned through apprenticeship and passed down over generations, this spirit of mentorship continues today, with teachers and students learning from one another through formal undergraduate and graduate programs, as well as more informal workshops. Designers might work directly with fabricators to bring their ideas to life. Others partake

42 — Christian Högstedt, *Lamellae Twisted Cuff* for Georg Jensen by Zaha Hadid Design, 2016.

43 — Iwan Baan, Heydar Aliyev Cultural Centre designed by Zaha Hadid Architects, Baku, Azerbaijan, 2013.

in the entire process, from design to creation, or collaborate with a small team. No matter the method, these artists bring a creative spirit to jewelry making that is not separate from, but closely aligned with, the broader art world.

44 — Eugène Fontenay, necklace, about 1875. Gold.

Working in Paris, Eugène Fontenay took inspiration from Hellenic Greek necklaces to create this fringe design. Instead of copying historical works of art, however, he combined motifs from various periods and cultures to create a piece rooted in the past, yet unique to the nineteenth century.

45 (OPPOSITE) — Marcus & Co.,
necklace, about 1905. Gold, platinum,
peridot, diamond, pearl, and enamel.

When Marcus & Co. made this necklace,
the company rivaled Tiffany & Co. as
America's premier jewelry house. This
Gilded Age jewel, with its undulating
lines and green plique-à-jour enamel,
pays homage to the European Art
Nouveau movement.

46 — Jaques and Marcus (later Marcus
& Co.), sketch for custom pendant,
about 1890–1910.

47 — Paul Lienard, *Seaweed*, about 1908.
Gold and pearl.

This elegant and simple design, with
whiplash curves surrounding a mabe
pearl, understates its outstanding
craftsmanship. Paul Liénard used a similar
motif in his graphic designs for the
fin-de-siècle jewelry magazine *Revue de
la bijouterie, joaillerie, orfèvrerie* (Review
of jewelry, fine jewelry, and metalwork).

48 — John Paul Cooper, *Big Double Gold*, 1908. Gold, abalone, tourmaline, moonstone, pearl, amethyst, and chrysoprase.

An architect, designer, and metalsmith, John Paul Cooper was a leading figure of the British Arts and Crafts movement. Working as head of the Metalwork Department of the Birmingham Municipal Art School from 1901 to 1906, Cooper instructed that metal and gemstones should "play on one another as two notes of music."[15]

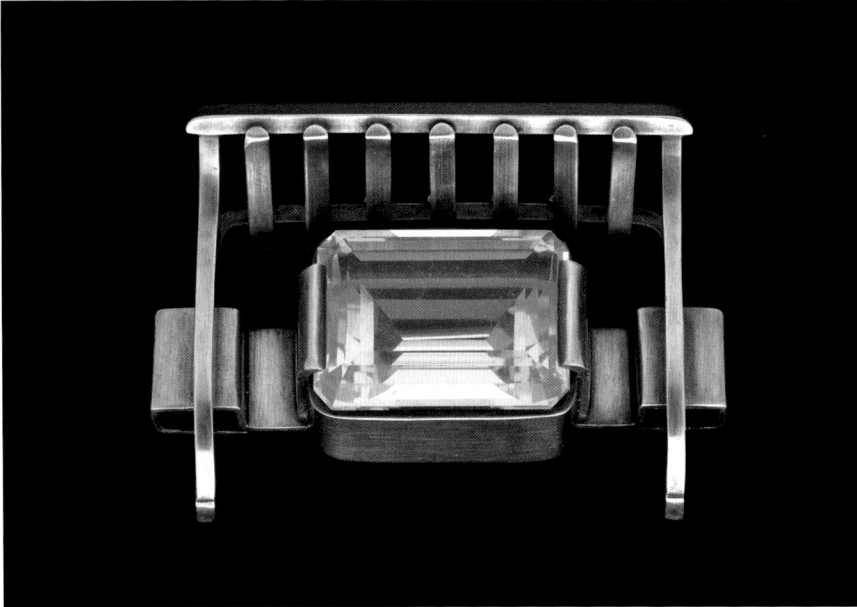

49 — Margret Craver, brooch, about 1945. Silver and quartz.

Margret Craver described this architectural brooch as representing a turning point in her career. In the years around World War II, Craver was one of the most important silversmiths in the United States, training veterans in the therapeutic work of metalsmithing.

50 — Margaret De Patta, ring, 1947–48. Gold and tourmalinated quartz.

Embodying Chicago's New Bauhaus concepts, this ring combines asymmetrical geometric forms with an unusual quartz gemstone embedded with spiky strands of black tourmaline. De Patta, a student of Lázló Moholy-Nagy, played with forms and concepts beyond those traditionally used in jewelry making.

51 — Claire Falkenstein, ring, about 1955.
Silver and glass.

Though better known as a sculptor, Claire Falkenstein was among the first jewelers to embrace Abstract Expressionism. This large ring—which resembles a figure with its right arm extended, as if gesturing to stop or throwing a punch—is equally at home on the finger, or standing on its own as a small sculpture.

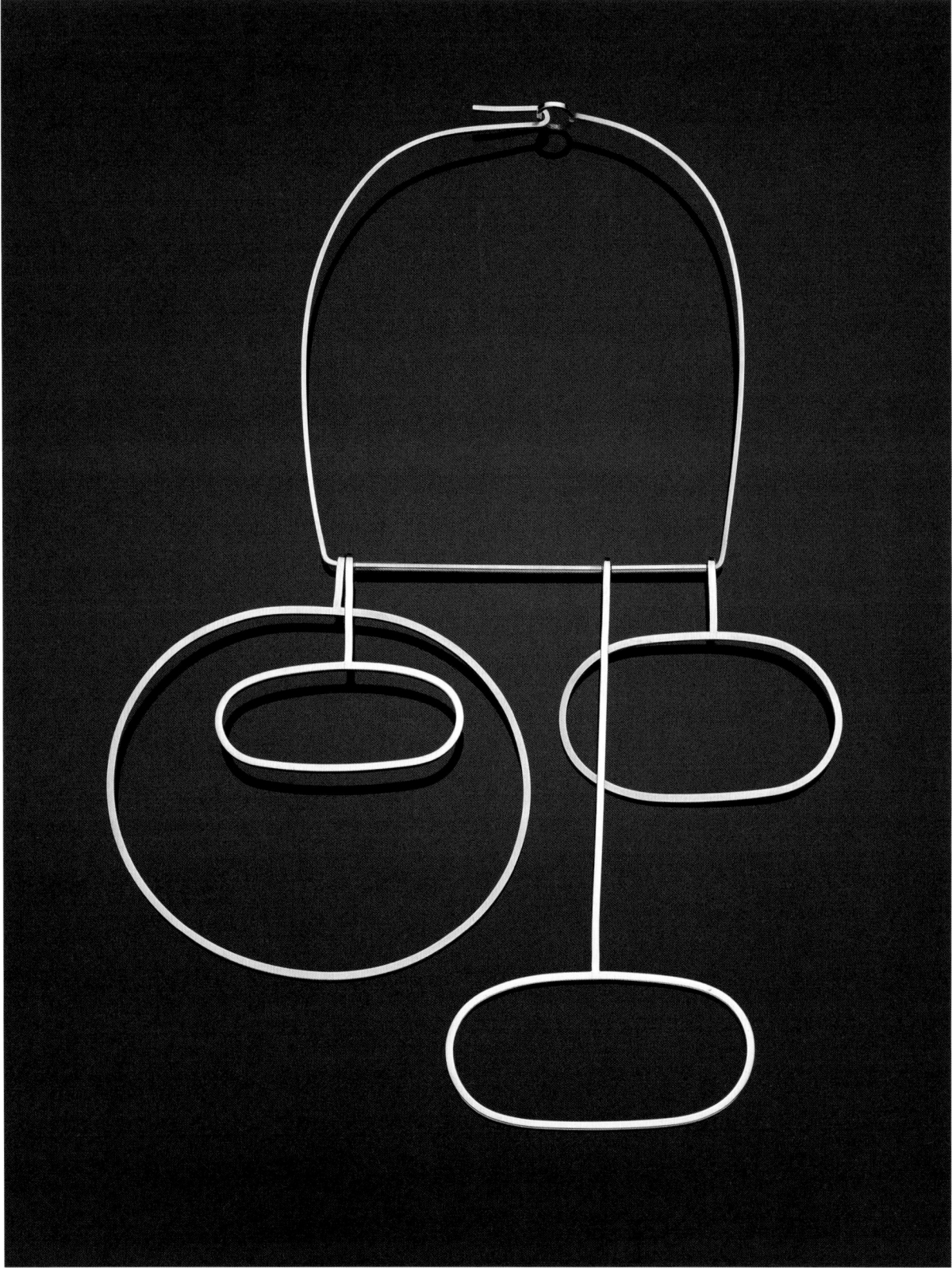

52 (OPPOSITE) — Betty Cooke, necklace, about 1959. Silver.

The deceptively simple jewelry of minimalist artist Betty Cooke conceals its technical perfection. Her necklaces are like drawings. The artist described, "We used to study what can be done with one straight line. I can spend years with a circle."[16] Cooke's jewelry was sold at her Baltimore shop, The Store Ltd, from its opening in 1965 until shortly after her death in 2024.

53 — Miyé Matsukata, necklace, about 1970–75. Silver, jade, agate, and carnelian.

Miyé Matsukata studied at the School of the Museum of Fine Arts, Boston, in the 1940s, and by the 1970s—when this necklace was made—her work was featured at Joan Sonnabend's Sculpture to Wear gallery in New York, alongside jewelry by artists such as Alexander Calder and Pablo Picasso.

54 — Niki de Saint Phalle and Adolfo Del Vivo for GEM Montebello, *Nana*, 1973. Gold and enamel.

Niki de Saint Phalle first introduced the curvaceous, colorful, exuberant *Nana* in the mid-1960s as a celebration of women's empowerment and motherhood. In the decades that followed, *Nana* was reproduced in various media and sizes. The feminist symbol—named after a French slang term for a young woman— can be worn as a pendant or a brooch.

55 (OPPOSITE) — Fuset y Grau, *Girl Blowing Bubbles*, about 1910. Gold, platinum, enamel, pearl, ivory, sapphire, and diamond.

In Spain, Barcelona was the center of the Art Nouveau movement. An outstanding example of the Catalan style, this plique-à-jour enamel pendant—which features a woman standing in front of a stained-glass window, blowing pearl bubbles— is more restrained than other Art Nouveau jewels created in France and Belgium at the time.

From 1939 to 1943, Harry Bertoia stood among the vanguard of mid-century modernism as head of the metal workshop at Michigan's Cranbrook Academy of Art. Bertoia worked in a variety of forms and scales, but during the war years, when metal use was restricted, he focused on smaller jewelry objects, which he gave as gifts to artist-friends like Charles and Ray Eames, as well as members of the Saarinen family.

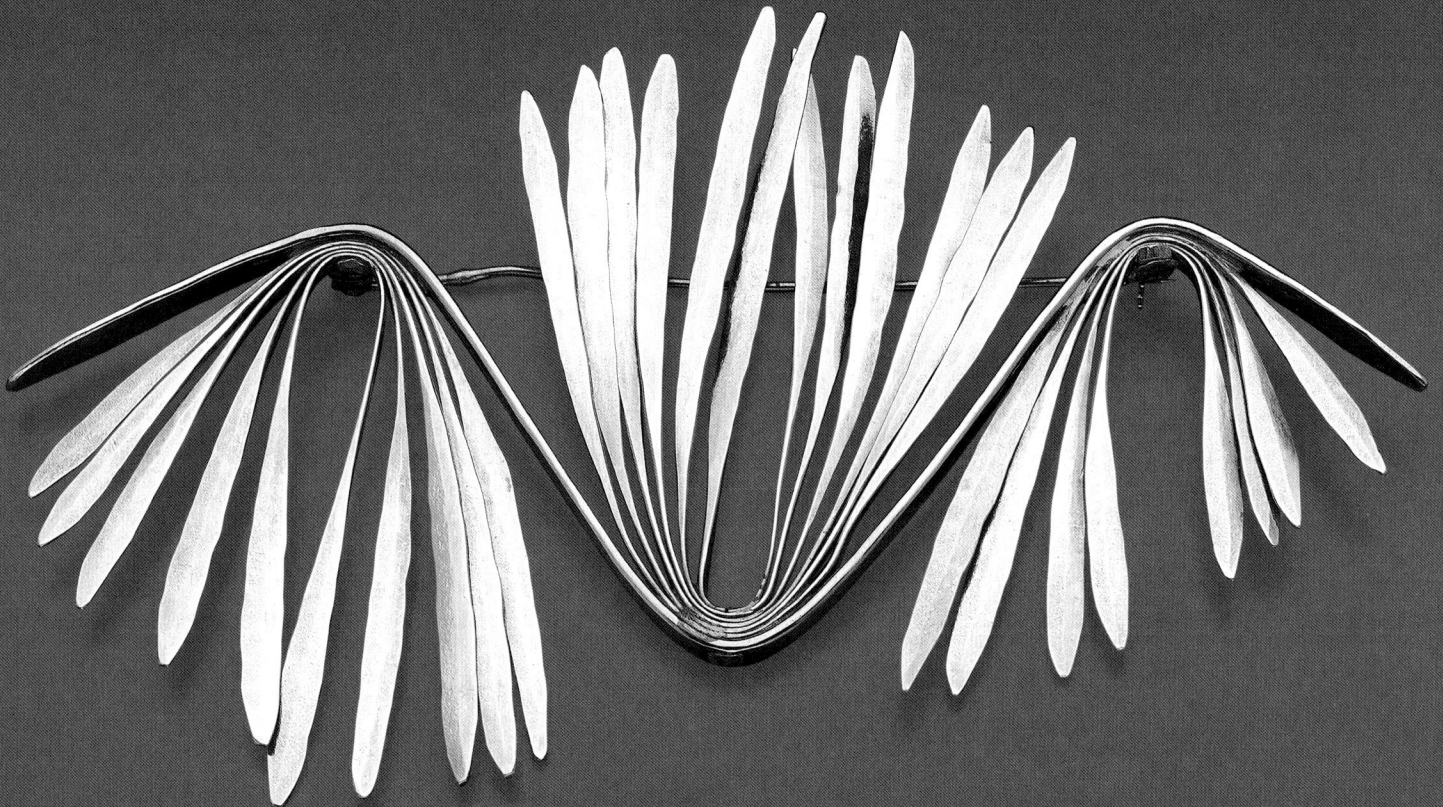

Sondra Sherman is a painter and jewelry
maker who is drawn to jewelry's personal
and emotional implications. She created
this bracelet, one of three in a series, to
respond to the body. When worn on the
wrist, this hinged bracelet can alternate
between flat and sculptural forms.

58 (OPPOSITE) — Manfred Bischoff, *The Comedian and the Martyr*, 1990. Gold, silver, and coral.

Comedy and philosophy come together in this enigmatic brooch by Manfred Bischoff. The artist's jewelry is often described as Surrealist, or as small sculpture. His combinations of witty titles and amorphous shapes leave his pieces open to interpretation, and they can almost be read like poetry.

59 — Peter Chang, brooch, about 1991. Acrylic and metal.

Peter Chang took inspiration from his youth in 1960s Liverpool to create plastic jewelry inspired by Pop Art. Exploring the outer limits of acrylic during the 1980s, Chang applied traditional art-making techniques like carving and inlay to plastic.

60 — Stanley Lechtzin, *Torque #25D*, 1972. Silver and resin.

This necklace balances history and innovation, blending Stanley Lechtzin's pioneering use of electroforming with his reverence for ancient jewelry designs. The torque style alludes to heavy metal ornaments worn by the Celts and Gauls, but the combination of plastic and electroformed silver adds a modern, lightweight dimension to the piece.

61 — Seulgi Kwon, *Blue Breath*, 2017. Silicone, pigment, thread, plastic, and feather.

At first glance, Korean artist Seulgi Kwon's luminous large-scale jewelry looks like glass sculpture. As soon as you touch it, however, you are met with a surprise: it's squishy! Made of silicone, a flexible material that is soft, light, and transparent, *Blue Breath* and other sculptural forms by Kwon evoke the biorhythms of plant life.

62 — Robert Ebendorf, *Man and His Pet Bee*, 1968. Copper, silver, tintype photograph, glass, brass, aluminum, and other found objects.

Inspired by Dadaism and part of a generation of jewelry artists increasingly interested in the narrative qualities of jewelry, Robert "Bob" Ebendorf was among the first jewelers to incorporate found objects in his work. To make this brooch, he juxtaposed a tintype photograph and a vintage kitchen timer with metalwork and beading.

63 (OPPOSITE) — Bettina Speckner, *Daphne*, 2007. Silver, tintype photograph, coral, and maple.

In *Daphne*, Bettina Speckner transforms a tintype photograph into a gem. The symbolic title derives from Greek mythology, where Daphne, a nymph who rejects the advances of suitors—including the god Apollo—is transformed into a laurel tree to escape her admirers. The reverse of the brooch features a meandering hand-carved vine.

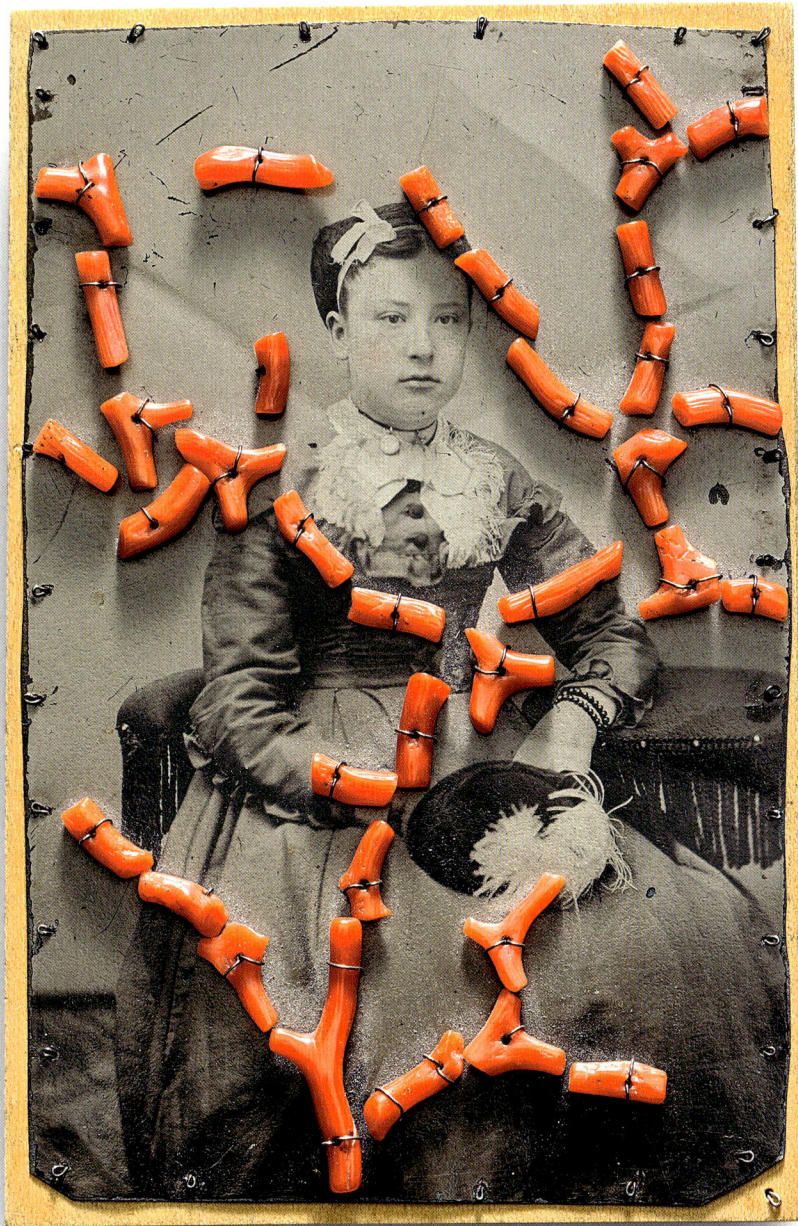

64 (OPPOSITE) — Kat Cole, *Old Lines*,
2016. Steel and enamel.

Contemporary artist Kat Cole reproduced
historical maps of Dallas, Texas, in black
and white enamel on the surface of this
necklace, part of her *Oil & Water* series.
When viewed from a distance, the pattern
is abstract; up close, the topology
becomes clear, inviting conversation on the
effects of human intervention on the
environment and the cities we call home.

65 — Zachery Lechtenberg, *Sweet Hearts*,
2019. Copper, silver, steel, and enamel.

The playful, Pop Art style of Zachery
Lechtenberg conceals his technical
prowess. Simultaneously comical and
unsettling, his jewelry is filled with
nostalgia for the 1980s and 1990s: namely
the comic books, trading cards, and
skateboarding equipment of his youth.
After working out his designs on paper,
Lechtenberg meticulously translates
his polychrome drawings to metal using
champlevé enamel.

66 — Feng J, *Blue Anthurium*, 2021. Gold, Paraiba tourmaline, aquamarine, spinel, sapphire, and diamond.

The dreamy landscapes and subtle palettes of French Impressionist artists informed the colors Feng J chose for this brooch. Painted with gemstones, the jeweler's design combines an invisible "floating" setting with gently colored electroplated gold, made to complement the stones and disappear into the background.

HATHOR-HEADED CRYSTAL PENDANT

YASMIN HEMMERLE

C ertain visuals and symbols in one's life, upon reflection, act as signposts for turning points in their story. A multigenerational heirloom, a picture of an ancestor, the first memory of kindness, the protective power of a familial bond. As an Egyptian, I have always been drawn to the phenomenal cultural legacy of my country: the richness of my heritage and the awe-inspiring achievements of its civilization.

As a child, I marveled at the creations of the pharaohs, but it wasn't until later in life that I began to fully appreciate the depth and forward-thinking nature of their society. From advancements in astrology, jewelry, medicine, and craft, to their profound understanding of physics and the importance of women, the ancient Egyptians were truly ahead of their time. Their jewelry, in particular, has always been a source of inspiration for me.

Beyond its visual allure, it is the profound meaning and thought embedded in each piece that fascinates me—now more than ever. One such piece is a hathor-headed crystal pendant, known as the *Head of Hathor*, a highly valued symbol of a multifaceted Egyptian goddess (FIG. 67).

The nearly 2,700-year-old crystal pendant was discovered in the tomb of queens from the eighth-century reign of Piankhy. Hathor is depicted in masterful detail above a rock crystal sphere, her face crafted out of gold and adorned with an elaborate collar, headdress, sun disk, and pair of cow's horns, as well as a protective uraeus cobra on her brow to signify her royalty. As a wife to Horus, the goddess represented loyalty, harmony, and the complementary energies that uphold balance and cosmic order. Their divine partnership showcased an

ideal of marital unity that transcended mere mortal relationships. In ancient Egypt, marriage was more than a union; it was a reflection of cosmic harmony. Hathor and Horus's relationship was not just about romance, but also about mutual respect and support, which were essential for maintaining Ma'at, the concept of truth, balance, and order.

The intricate craftsmanship of this treasure also reflects the advanced skills of ancient Egyptian artisans, who were not merely creators of beautiful objects, but part of the spiritual practice of imbuing such artifacts with reverence. The materials they used, such as gold and semiprecious stones, were chosen for their symbolic meanings as well as their beauty. Gold, representing the flesh of the gods, adds layers of significance to the pendant. It stands as a testament to the ancient Egyptians' ability to weave together art, spirituality, and daily life into a cohesive and meaningful whole.

As illustrated by this pendant, Hathor was often depicted with a human face and cow ears, or horns. This unique imagery reinforces her role as a provider of well-being and abundance, as cows were highly valued in ancient Egypt for their ability to produce milk—a dietary staple—and as symbols of fertility and nourishment. By embodying these traits, Hathor ensured the land's fertility and the people's prosperity, symbols of her life-sustaining power.

The goddess also promoted joy, compassion, and emotional healing, fostering connections through her divine affection that transcended time and space. Love, in the context

BRILLIANCE

of Hathor's worship, was not merely romantic, but encompassed all forms of meaningful relationships. Her temples were centers of joy and celebration, where music, dance, and festivities were common, reflecting her association with pleasure and happiness. Hathor's influence encouraged people to form bonds based on mutual respect and genuine affection, thus strengthening the social fabric of ancient Egyptian communities.

Hathor was a fierce and unwavering protector, safeguarding her devotees from harm and leading them through life's challenges with strength and compassion. This protective nature was deeply intertwined with the goddess's role as a mother. She epitomized motherhood through her protective, loving essence, symbolizing fertility and birth, and embodying the cycle of creation and rebirth. Her maternal care extended beyond her immediate family: she was often depicted as the mother of all pharaohs, guiding them as they fulfilled their divine roles on earth.

As a mother myself, I resonate with Hathor's nurturing and protective qualities. The act of giving and nurturing life is an experience that connects me to the ancient wisdom and strength she embodies. Under the goddess's watchful eye, every moment spent caring for my family can be seen as a reflection of the eternal cycle of creation and rebirth. In this role, I find strength and purpose, much like Hathor, in ensuring the well-being and growth of my loved ones. I see Hathor as a representation of all mothers and women around the world who have relentlessly fostered life through the eons—a humbling and rather emotional realization.

Hathor's representation of women is especially significant when viewed through a modern lens; in ancient Egypt, the awarding of such high respect to a goddess was ground-breaking. In a society that primarily revered women for their essential role in life, Hathor's example was pioneering. She demonstrated that femininity was not a single quality, but a tapestry of attributes, including intelligence, compassion, and inner strength. Through her, women in ancient Egypt found a powerful role model who validated their diverse contributions to society. Her multi-faceted nature reflects the complexity, power, and resilience of women.

The Hathor pendant in the collection of the MFA Boston serves as a testament to these myriad attributes. Worn as a form of protection and blessing, the necklace was believed to carry the goddess's power and benevolence. Both men and women wore such amulets, seeking Hathor's guidance and favor in their daily lives. Such ceremonial objects are something we have also embraced in contemporary society; jewelry in particular is associated with talismanic symbols of joy and protection, as well as personal adornment, in our quest for self-expression and self-discovery.

As part of a fourth-generation jewelry house, where I work alongside my husband, Christian Hemmerle, as well as his parents, Stefan and Sylveli, I am deeply inspired by the intricate crafts-manship and symbolic meanings of such pieces. The act of creating jewelry is not merely about aesthetics; it is about infusing each piece with intention and narrative. The Hathor amulet represents the pinnacle of this art form. It is a reminder that jewelry can be a powerful conduit for expressing and connecting with the wearer—and a conduit for something spiritual, too. It has moved me on several levels, and reflecting on the Hathor pendant has reinvigorated my quest to find Ma'at—the ancient Egyptian value of harmony and balance.

As we delve deeper into the stories and symbols of our past, we discover not only the richness of our heritage, but also the timeless lessons that continue to resonate with us, guiding us in our own lives and reminding us of the eternal cycles of love, protection, and creation that define our existence.

CHICLET NECKLACE AND MOSAIC CUFF

HENRIETTA LIDCHI

Jewelry as an art form is distinguished by two essential qualities. The first is that it is worn on the body. As intimate sculpture, jewelry affects our physical senses—it weighs or sounds or glistens—a tacit admission of the human need to be adorned. The second is the idea of preciousness. Jewelry is universally made of precious materials, but what constitutes preciousness is culturally subjective. It's possible the only way of coming to a shared understanding of preciousness as an idea is some form of equation between effort and rarity, with the addition of emotional attachment—all of which may be influenced by geography, culture, and patterns of availability.

Materials are at the heart of what makes Angie Reano Owen's jewelry fascinating and seductive. Owen's distinctive contribution to the aesthetic register of traditional jewelry from Santo Domingo Pueblo came into view in the 1970s and 1980s. Her innovation lay in reviving ancestral Puebloan mosaic work made entirely of shell and stone in two distinct, innovative patterns: herringbone and stepped. Mosaic is a painstaking technique demanding a profound understanding of materials: how to cut stone to get the best slivers and brightest colors, how to draw on the natural shape of shells used as backing. Owen builds intricate patterns across curved surfaces using epoxy and pins, her signature herringbone style greedily demanding material. The most perilous stage of the process comes near the end, when she grinds the rough mosaic to a unified, smooth, and polished surface. The silky surface, tangible weight, and color combinations lend a sensuousness to her work.

Santo Domingo Pueblo, or Kewa Pueblo, the Native American community to which Owen belongs, is a center of lapidary work in New Mexico with a long history of trading jewelry of worked shell and stone. Owen comes from a family of jewelers. One of eight children, she grew up in a household where her mother and father, Clara and Joe Isidiro Reano, made jewelry, and their children learned the craft through patient observation, starting with small technical tasks as they pursued their schooling. The family's jewelry spanned a variety of forms: Owen witnessed the diversity of work they made for the community and Diné (Navajo) customers, as well as to sell to museums and non-Native tourists. For the community, the family made shell heishi necklaces. For Diné clients, Owen's parents made jaclahs, elegant and necessary ear pendants of graduated turquoise beads and corn-shaped tabs of shell, gypsum, and spiny oyster. For museums, her mother created small turquoise and shell mosaic earrings on cottonwood, a style Owen also produced at the beginning of her career.

The family also made Thunderbird-style necklaces and earrings. This Santo Domingo form, which arose during the Great Depression, answered tourists' desire for locally made and affordable souvenirs along the railroad. Now recognized as an important jewelry tradition, Thunderbird jewelry was a creative response to economic stricture which made use of the centuries-old tradition of Pueblo mosaic work. In these Thunderbird pieces, more expensive natural materials were simply substituted with upcycled ones.

The Reano family cut up and combined recycled records, batteries, and colorful plastic combs and headbands from Woolworth with small pieces of turquoise adhered with pitch, or epoxy, mixed with soot for color. Owen remembers her father bringing black battery casings harvested from junk yards in Albuquerque.[1] She recalls him fondly for his wisdom and innovations. Joe Isidiro Reano developed time-saving ways to cut up and flatten batteries, and mechanized the process of making beads and tabs. Owen's mother, Clara Reano, the family's provider as farmer, cook, and jeweler, worked tirelessly with her children, making around fifty necklaces a week to sell under the Portal at the Palace of the Governors in Santa Fe on Saturdays. Owen grew up in the Native American Art business, learning from her grandmother, Monica Silva, a Santa Clara potter, skilled artist, and successful businesswoman who married into Santo Domingo Pueblo. By the age of eleven, Owen was traveling by train with her grandmother to the Flagstaff All-Indian Pow Wow in Arizona, which ran from 1929 to 1979, to sell the family's work. By eighteen, she was traveling alone.

Owen's distinctive artistic voice matured in the 1970s, when Santa Fe was a destination for those looking for counterculture, and ambitious young traders entered the jewelry business, running their own small shops. Owen witnessed this transformative moment in the Native American art business, and supplied work drawing on the breadth of her experience, as well as her special skill and eye for mosaic. Her stories of this juncture are historically important and endlessly entertaining. A key moment in the evolution of Owen's work was a visit to the Arizona State Museum in Tucson, where she saw the boundless sophistication of Hohokam jewelry firsthand: *Glycymeris* shell bracelets, inlay, mosaic, and carved work of shell, turquoise, jet, abalone, and spiny oyster backed onto shell and cottonwood. She responded by creating her own unique style of mosaic jewelry: iconic cuffs and bangles, backed on tiger cowrie or Glycymeris shell, dominated by sky-blue or green turquoise combined with traditional materials of jet, spiny oyster, and mother-of-pearl, or coral and lapis.

When recently asked about her patterning, Owen answered that it is guided by the need to bring out the color of each stone, "It is the turquoise that chooses you.... If you have very little green turquoise, then you put in lots of colors. At least, that is how it dictates to me." Looking at her bracelets in the MFA's collection, Owen noted, "You have to go along with the stone," sometimes using lighter stones or shells, like mother of pearl, next to the intense blue to "chill off the turquoise" (FIG. 69).

In the 1980s, Owen developed the chiclet necklace, one of her most popular styles, a multi-stranded form with mosaic cubes backed onto an abalone shell (FIG. 68). Her most accomplished piece in the collection is a five-strand necklace of clamshell heishi interspersed with tear-shaped tabs—reminiscent of Owen's earrings—and a central olla-shaped pendant. The mosaic of matched Chinese turquoise and coral follows the gentle curve of the abalone shell backing. There are only three of these in existence.

For Owen, material is her guide. Her genuineness of intention is the guarantee of success. Modesty and generosity are central to her artistic practice. As a collector, she has often traded her work with fellow artists. As an artist, she continues to make a range of work, despite her many accomplishments. Owen inherited this principle from her father, who advocated that she should always have a pair of "teeny weeny earrings so that a person who does not have any money, or not much, could own...my work."

68 (OPPOSITE, TOP)— Angie Reano Owen, chiclet necklace, 1993. Turquoise, coral, mother of pearl, lapis lazuli, spiny oyster, and silver.

69 (OPPOSITE, BOTTOM)— Angie Reano Owen, mosaic cuff, 1995. Tiger cowrie, turquoise, spiny oyster, mother-of-pearl, jet, and epoxy.

FOREVER DANCING—
BRIGHT STAR

MELANIE GRANT

F orever Dancing—Bright Star is not a brooch. Instead, it is the reincarnation of a real butterfly, hermetically sealed between shimmering rock crystal and mother-of-pearl, supported by a titanium skeleton, and carved with poetic lightness by artist and sculptor Wallace Chan (FIG. 70). The delicate, powdery scales of each wing are preserved in a vacuum so that light and shadow can be teased to the surface through expert carving to create an explosion of vibrant color. Its construction took three long years and, in its creation, Chan allowed the butterfly to live again. "'Forever Dancing' (我還在飛舞), if literally translated from the Chinese, means 'I am still dancing,'" says Chan of his jewel. "To give a new life to what no longer lives in the form of art, her once short-lived beauty is now encapsulated with stones that will outlive us all."[1]

Gifted to the MFA in February 2023 by Christin Xing and Rex Wong, two collectors of Chan's work, this piece is a symbol of undying love, an eternal blessing, and a token of friendship. It pays homage to the fourth-century classical Chinese philosophy of Zhuangzi, author of one of the two fundamental texts of Taoism, who believed that the greatest of all happiness can be found in the belief that "all is one." In his ancient manuscript, he recalled a dream where he was fluttering about as a butterfly, merrily doing as he pleased. He awoke with a jolt as himself, but he didn't know if he was a butterfly dreaming he was a man, or a man dreaming he was a butterfly. He called this state of being the "Transformation of Things," and concluded that the difference between reality and dreams was irrelevant.

Wallace Chan is a man who also travels freely between worlds, who believes that the subjective categories we place ourselves in are limiting. To Chan, we are all interconnected—each of us is "as small and as big as every other existence." Engaging with this notion in his artistic practice, he has made hundreds of intricate bejeweled butterflies since 2010, when he debuted his first titanium art piece at the Swiss jewelry show Baselworld. While there, people began calling him "the Butterfly Man from China." The name stuck, like a swallowtail butterfly to nectar.

Now resting in the MFA's permanent collection, the journey of *Forever Dancing—Bright Star* feels complete. In a conversation I had with Chan while writing this essay, the artist reflected, "A museum is a house of muses. I visit museums to be educated and inspired—and also to dream. It is an honor to have my works alongside the great minds in history." I wondered aloud: if he took a leaf out of Zhuangzi's book and became a butterfly himself—even for a day, or even for a dream—what would he do? Where would he go? "I would go where the butterfly goes," he said—which makes total sense in the creative utopia that is the Wallace Chan universe.

70 — Wallace Chan, *Forever Dancing—
Bright Star*, 2013. Diamond, rock crystal,
mother-of-pearl, butterfly specimen,
pearl, and titanium.

71 — BHAGAT, *Jali*, 2024. Gold, emerald, and diamond.

JALI

AMIN JAFFER

I first met Viren Bhagat in 1993, just after he had decided to turn his hand to jewelry design with the encouragement of Gianni Bulgari, whose bold gold creations provided early inspiration for his work. A fourth-generation jeweler based in Mumbai, the artist works with his sons Varun and Jay under the eponymous brand name BHAGAT. Growing up in a Gujarati jewelry making and trading family, he drew particular inspiration from his father, a talented artist and art school teacher from whom he learned draftsmanship; a cluster of perfectly sharpened pencils and pads of paper are staples of Bhagat's desk. During my first visit to his atelier, I was struck by his totally original use of old-cut diamonds, set in bold and imaginative ways.

A 2024 gold, emerald, and diamond brooch by BHAGAT takes the form of a *jali*, a type of per-forated screen used to divide space in traditional Indian architecture (FIG. 71). Admitting air while restricting direct light and view, *jalis* were traditionally used for windows, and for defining spaces that inter-mediated between the exterior and interior (SEE FIG. 72). At their most sophisticated, such screens were composed of complex, repeated patterns, whether geometric, abstract, or drawing on naturalistic foliate designs. Outstanding examples can be found in Sultanate and Mughal architecture, such as the Mosque of Sidi Saiyyed in Ahmedabad, the Tomb of Humayun in Delhi, and the Tomb of Salim Chishti in the Jammi Masjid at Fatehpur Sikri.

The pointed arch of the *jali* is a form synonymous with sacred and secular architecture in the Islamic world. Portals of this shape defined the great mosque, palace, and mausoleum complexes of the Muslim dynasties that ruled over much of India in the early modern period, such as at the Illuminated Tomb of the Mughal empress Mumtaz Mahal, known today as the Taj Mahal. Both symbolically and within an architectural context, an archway represents an opening, inviting viewers to look through and beyond.

The jeweler's choice of diamonds and emeralds further supports the symbolism of this arched *jali*. Specially cut diamond apertures are calculated to reflect light, associ-ated as it is with divinity across religions—exemplified in the Qur'anic phrase, "God is the light of the heavens and the earth."[1] The gems themselves also add layers of meaning: from ancient times until their discovery in Brazil in the early eighteenth century, diamonds from India were among the principal adornments on rings, bracelets, necklaces, and crowns worn as tokens of love and power across the world. In ancient Indian treatises on gemstones, diamonds were associated with divine power and protection, thanks to their clarity and dura-bility. The hardness of diamonds—whose name derives from the ancient Greek *adamas*, or "strong"—has rendered this gemstone a symbol of eternity across civilizations.

Surrounding the diamonds are cabochon emeralds, set in a barely-visible gold frame. The gems represent the color of peace in Islam, evocative of the garden—and by extension, of paradise. Given the significance of green to Muslims—it is believed to have been the favorite color of the Prophet

72 — Gateway, Indian, about 1677.
Red sandstone.

Mohamed—emeralds enjoyed a privileged position in Islamic India, playing a symbolic role in royal jewelry. Their supply accompanied the opening of maritime routes across the Atlantic, Pacific, and Indian Oceans, when emeralds from Colombian mines—then under Spanish rule—were brought to South Asia, where they were amassed and worn, whether as beads or faceted, carved, and engraved with dynastic inscriptions or prayers.

Both diamonds and emeralds played an important role in the early modern maritime global economy, binding Western commercial powers to Indian markets. Indian diamonds served as a concentrated form of wealth that could be more securely and easily moved from South Asia to Europe than gold or silver bullion. Emeralds from Colombia were one of the commodities used by Europeans to settle the trade imbalance experienced by seventeenth- and eighteenth-century Western trading powers operating in India, which supplied their insatiable demand for the spices necessary for the European diet, and for dyeing plain, printed, and woven cotton fabrics. The supply of emeralds helped to stem the drain of bullion from European economies to pay for these Indian products, which became essential adornments for Westerners.

These strong historic references are a hallmark of the artist's work. As in this brooch, his forms are often inspired by Mughal architecture and decorative arts, or by uniquely complex traditional Indian ornaments such as forehead, turban, and hair ornaments as well as upper armbands and anklets. Bhagat's mounts sometimes recall more contemporary influences, including European jewelry of the 1920s and 1930s, an era whose designs exercise a strong influence over Bhagat's taste—particularly the Art Deco and Modernist creations of European and North American jewelry houses for Indian princes, who during the period sought to refresh their ancestral jewels by having them reset in the latest Western styles, shunning more traditional yellow gold for lighter and stronger platinum mounts.

What makes Bhagat's creations original is his reinterpretation of these historical elements. Characteristics of typical Indian jewelry, such as floral and vegetal forms, the crescent moon, or tassels of pearls and diamonds, are interpreted in a refined, abstracted, and ethereal way using specially calibrated gems, most often flat diamonds. And while traditional Indian jewelry is known for its rich polychromy—whether in the use of enamel or the combination of colored stones with yellow gold—Bhagat often sets his gems in reduced, monochrome palettes, sometimes composed solely of diamonds and pearls, or married with a single type of colored gem. This simplified range of colors is further underlined by the use of minimal—often invisible—platinum and gold mounts, the latter evident on this brooch. The irregular shapes and inimitable patina of the old diamonds and colored stones that Bhaghat uses lend a softness to his often architectural and ambitious forms.

Operating from a principal location in Mumbai and a second in London, and without resorting to any advertising, Viren Bhagat's eponymous brand has transformed the world's idea of high-level jewelry from India, giving it a contemporary identity, one which honors the past but is entirely original in its effect.

BODY
AS CANVAS

A piece of jewelry is in a sense an object that is not complete in itself. Jewelry is a "whatisit?" until you relate it to the body.
—Art Smith[1]

J ewelry is an essential component of style. A sartorial choice, jewelry is a core element of dress—like all other accessories, from shoes and hats to handbags, it aids in the creation of a look. Even so, it is more often studied from the perspective of the decorative arts than from a fashion lens. Jewelry, however, doesn't fully function without the body. The human form is the armature—the canvas—for the jeweler's art. Dutch art historian Marjan Unger described how jewelry functions simultaneously as "an object that is worn on the human body" and "as a decorative and symbolic addition to its outward appearance."[2] While that may seem like an obvious definition, some artists create without thinking about wearability, and in the museum context, the body has rarely been considered. Yet, the human form is where jewelry comes to life. In both humble and extravagant ways, jewelry exists as part of an ensemble.

Actress Claudette Colbert had recently won an Academy Award for her role in *It Happened One Night* and was the highest-paid woman in the United States when she likely encountered a starfish brooch in Boivin's atelier on Avenue de la Opéra in Paris in 1938 (FIG. 74).[3] Colbert was visiting the city of her birth for the first time in years and, despite telling the media she had no intention of shopping, the life-size brooch must have captured her attention—she purchased it.[4] With its exceptional size, realistic design, and unique shape, the starfish was an avant-garde choice for Colbert, who was known for her conservative style. As Colbert told the *Boston Globe* in 1940, "When you become a motion picture star, you have to behave like one."[5] Boivin's brooch was indeed the pinnacle of *style moderne*, and it occupied the space between haute *joaillerie* and haute couture.

Boivin's starfish demonstrates the jeweler's technical mastery, and has since been described as among the best designs the firm ever produced.[6] The specific brooch purchased by Colbert was the first of four ruby and amethyst versions made under the direction of Jeanne Boivin by designer Juliette Moutard; later, the brooch was also produced in emerald and aquamarine. The starfish is lifelike in both its scale and its movement, with many small hinges enabling each of its five limbs to flex in the same manner as the marine creature. The bejeweled rays move up, down, and around to hug the curves of the body.

The jewelry house, founded by René Boivin in 1890 and managed after his 1917 death by his wife, Jeanne Boivin, also boasted close ties to the world of fashion—Jeanne's brother was famed couturier Paul Poiret. As the jeweler's biographer, Françoise Cailles, wrote, "To talk of clothes and finery is to talk of jewels. In jewelry, the fashion-conscious find their most prestigious—and most permanent—accessory, something adding luster both to the garment and the woman wearing it."[7] The starfish brooch proved no exception. Between its design and its display in Boivin's showroom, the gem appeared in American

73 — Alfred Eisenstaedt, Claudette Colbert wearing starfish brooch, 1938.

75 — Belt with buckle and seven plaques, Chinese, 8th century. Silver and jade.

fashion magazines: first as an illustration in *Vogue* in 1937, followed by a photograph in *Harper's Bazaar* the next year. Publications like these offered readers an enticing glimpse into the latest jewelry styles, and lifestyle magazines provided a peek into the lives and tastes of movie stars like Colbert. When the actress graced the page wearing Boivin's starfish brooch, she demonstrated the intersection of her careful styling and her most fashion-forward jewelry choice. In an unpublished portrait taken by *Life* magazine photographer Alfred Eisenstaedt in 1938, Colbert smiles coyly at the camera, the starfish brooch pinned to the collar of a short-sleeve dress (FIG. 73). In 1939, a writer for *Modern Screen* described Colbert wearing the brooch with a "green and garnet colored dress."[8] The actress wore it again later that year in a spread for *Photoplay*, pairing it with a short Persian lamb coat and jaunty hat.[9]

As adornment—placed on the head, worn through the ears, suspended from the neck, pinned to a jacket, or encircling a finger—jewelry is indelibly connected to the body, and with it, the clothes one wears. Whether functional or decorative, jewelry is an essential ingredient in creative expression, in the sartorial fashions of a time, place, or culture. Jewels are indicators of rank, status, and also of style. They are designed to decorate, seduce, sway and tremble, and generally radiate—and enhance—beauty. Jewelry can be functional, created to hold up or secure a garment. It might be made to endure, or—when paired with the rise of mass production and the introduction of ready-to-wear clothing—crafted to keep up with shifting fashions. On the body, jewelry becomes a powerful signifier, connecting it to ideals of beauty and themes of access and power.

As couturiere Gabrielle "Coco" Chanel quipped, "Luxury is a necessity that begins where necessity ends."[10] A belt, for example, designed to hold up a pair of pants or cinch the waistline of a dress. However, not all belts are created equal: while one sometimes needs a belt to stop their pants from slipping down their hips, at other times, the look of such an object supersedes its necessity. In this way, practical objects become decorative, luxury objects, where function is secondary to style. Take, for example, one belt in the MFA's collection: although all that remains today are seven jade plaques, traces of metal rivets on the reverse of each panel reveal that they would have been attached to a strip of leather. While the belt they adhered to likely served a use, these plaques are an exceptional indication of the type of luxury Chanel described (FIG. 75). Created more than 1,200 years ago, in the eighth century, they each feature a seated musician on each plaque, all of them wearing Central Asian clothing—hats, tunics, long trousers, and boots—and sitting cross-legged on the ground. The panel illustrations' rhythmic drapery, curving lines, and sense of energetic movement resembles Chinese Buddhist carvings as well as frescoes from the Tang Dynasty (618–907 CE).[11] When worn around the waist, the

76 — Fibulae, Kabylian, 19th century. Silver, enamel, and resin.

BRILLIANCE

belt likely projected a sense of authority and power: the wearer would have been figuratively and literally surrounded by musicians and attendants. Such a luxurious jade ornament was likely reserved for use by the emperor, royal family members, or high officials.

In Northern Africa, jewelry—mostly enameled silver—has also historically been used to secure garments (FIG. 76). Worn at the shoulder, an ornament such as a pair of fibulae would secure a cloak or scarf, the attached chain ensuring the garment remained in place. The fibulae in the MFA's collection were worn by Berber women in Algeria and, as is traditional for jewelry in North Africa and the broader Islamic world, likely made up an important part of a woman's dowry, given by prospective husbands as part of a marriage agreement. A form of portable wealth, these fibulae offered financial protection. In the late fifteenth century, a time when many Jewish people immigrated to North Africa to work as silversmiths, similar examples were made by Jewish craftspeople working in the region. The decorations would have added to ensembles that also included colorful patterned textiles, creating a strong visual effect. Nothing about their function requires fibulae to be artful, yet they are.

Jewelry can indeed offer a bit of color or sparkle to an ensemble. When viewed in the right light, diamonds and diamond-like materials glitter and provide a luminous, otherworldly effect. In the 1700s, large, glittering brooches, known as *devants de corsage*, were worn pinned to the chest (FIG. 77). At the time, fashionable dresses such as the *robe à la Française* opened in the front, and required a V-shaped panel known as a stomacher to conceal and decorate the functional closure. These small textiles were sumptuously decorated with silk embroidery and metal threads. For added sparkle, a brooch might have been worn over the stomacher to create a dazzling effect under candlelight.

78 — Alphonse Auger, corsage ornament, about 1890. Silver, gold, and diamond.

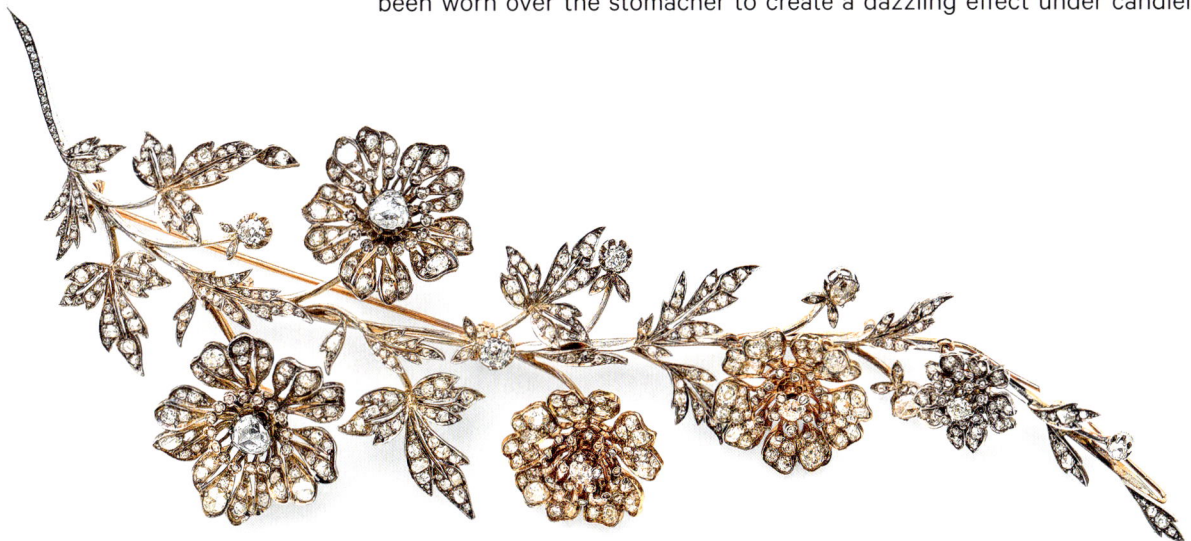

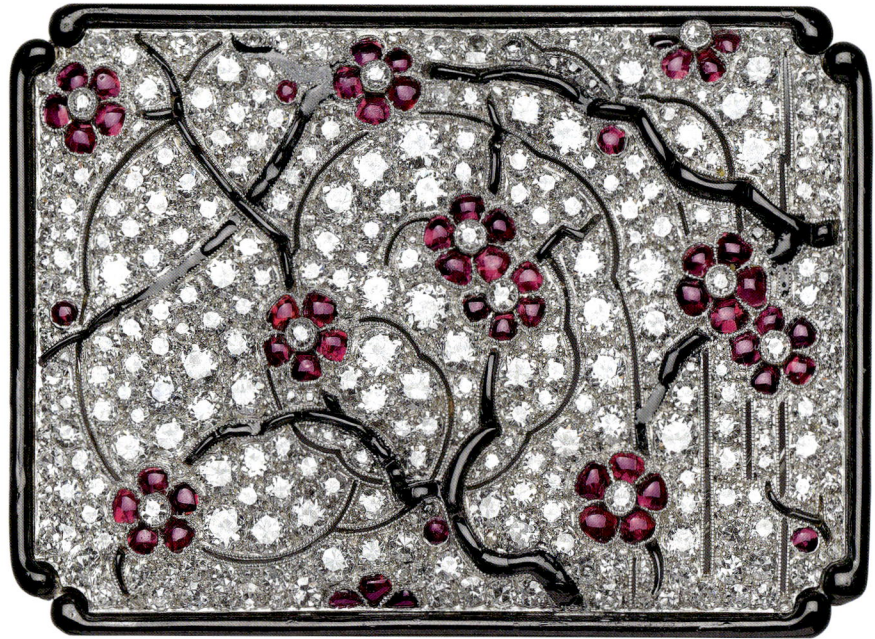

79 — Lacloche Frères, Japanesque brooch, about 1925. Platinum, gold, enamel, diamond, ruby, and onyx.

80 — Hay Wrightson for Raphael Tuck & Sons, *Queen Mary*, about 1920.

The reverse of one brooch in the MFA's collection has large, flat loops, allowing the gem to be attached to a garment or a ribbon. Stomachers largely fell out of fashion in major cities by the close of the eighteenth century, but they continued to be popular in Spanish provinces, like Navarre, in the Basque region.

In the nineteenth century, French jeweler Auger likely looked back at eighteenth-century *devant de corsage* (stomacher) styles to create his nine-inch brooch of a stylized branch of flowers (FIG. 78). Resembling white roses, the blossoms might have symbolized the virtue and charity of the wearer, their meaning taken from the popular 1819 French publication *Le Langage des fleurs* (The Language of Flowers), which codified the meanings behind the wearing or giving of certain flowers, offering a code for lovers and friends to decipher. Auger's brooch dates to a time of intense artistic interest in the natural world, but flowers, insects, and sea creatures have proven enduring inspirations among jewelry artists, their ephemeral nature made permanent in gemstones and precious metals. In 2024, *Vogue* editor-in-chief Anna Wintour wore a similar brooch to the Met Gala celebrating the opening of the exhibition *Sleeping Beauties: Reawakening Fashion*.

Brooches offer endless possibilities for wearers to express their sartorial style. A rectangular diamond, ruby, and onyx brooch, made around 1925 by French jeweler Lacloche Frères and once owned by Mary of Teck, wife of the British King George V, features a cherry blossom design (FIG. 79). While she preferred Art Nouveau's choker-style necklaces (known as *collier de chien*

81 — Lucien Lelong, *Flore*, 1925.

after the French word for dog collar), which Queen Mary paired with long sautoirs, or long necklaces, the brooch's quintessentially Art Deco–style design offered the monarch something au courant (FIG. 80). The rectangular design would have been quite easy to wear as a plaque, attached to a ribbon and worn around the neck. A more fashionable option would have been to pin it to the low-slung waistline of the era's ubiquitous little black dress (FIG. 81). Years after its creation, the monarch gifted the brooch to Angela Dowding on the occasion of her marriage to Mary's cousin, Gerald Laselles. A handwritten note on Marlborough House stationery reads: "For Angela from Mary R, 1952."[12]

Jewelry is often thought to be more enduring than fashion. Heirlooms are handed down from one generation to the next, and, for much of its history, jewelry was not considered with the clothing trends of the day in mind. However, there has always been jewelry that requires garments to function; with the advent of mass production and the rise of ready-to-wear clothing, jewelry, too, has become more directly connected to seasonal fashions. Innovations and changes to jewelry manufacturing corresponded to the establishment of standard sizing and the birth of department stores as one-stop fashion emporiums.

Beginning in the eighteenth century, a style of jewelry emerged that was less precious: as the Industrial Revolution expedited production, these mass-produced designs—called costume, or fashion, jewelry—became more stylistically bold and much less costly than fine jewelry.[13] Jewelers used cut steel to offer the effect of diamonds and either placed colored foils behind clear quartz or used glass and plastic to create the look of gemstones. By the twentieth century, more technological advances allowed such designs to respond to seasonal fashion changes. Showy, limited-production fashion jewelry was primarily made in Italy or France using glass beads or poured glass, and was presented by European fashion designers as part of their seasonal collections. In the United States, costume jewelry was largely designed in New York, mass-produced in southeastern Massachusetts and Providence, Rhode Island, and retailed by American department stores selling ready-to-wear garments.[14] Under American direction, costume jewelry embraced a three-pronged mix that simultaneously offered less expensive copies of fine gems, jewelry created in partnership with fashion designers, and novelty items that were colorful and fun. Regardless of its name or country of origin, these styles incorporated inexpensive metals and enamel, or glass or plastic gems. In all instances, it tended to be designed at a large scale, and worn layered or stacked for maximum visual effect.

In the early twentieth century, recently immigrated entrepreneurs to the United States founded firms in New York—including Coro, Trifari, and

82–83 (ABOVE AND OPPOSITE, TOP) —
Adolph Katz for Coro, *Duette*, 1944.
Gold-plated silver, glass, and enamel.

Schreiner—with the intent of creating styles to offer alongside American fashions. As costume jewelry gained popularity at the height of the Great Depression and in the years during and after World War II, these firms sold a wide range of styles that could be worn in creative ways. Coro and Trifari introduced double-clip brooches, marketed by Coro as *Duette* and Trifari as *Clip-Mates*, which could be worn as a single brooch or taken apart and worn as two dress clips (FIGS. 82–83).[15] Designs by Miriam Haskell and others also included clip

elements in their designs, offering clients an element of creativity and wearability (SEE FIG. 11).

Fashion jewelry created for French houses such as Chanel, Dior, and Lanvin was presented as part of their seasonal collections, and this association with fashion gave women greater autonomy over their choice of jewelry. Whether created to complement made-to-measure *haute couture* ensembles or sold as accessories in retail shops, this was not the type of jewelry one waited to receive as a gift; instead, it was affordable, accessible, and could be purchased with an eye to personal style. Its lack of preciousness made it no less important than jewelry created using platinum and diamonds, but its lower cost and positioning as fashion offered different considerations.

Jewelry was equally important at other French couture houses, where it was a key element of the industry's head-to-toe offerings. Gabrielle Chanel introduced a style that mingled this type of "fake" jewelry with "real" jewelry to great aplomb. Her own best model, Chanel wore what became her signature style of jewelry on her travels to Ravenna, Italy, which inspired the iconic Maltese cross cuff bracelets designed for the brand by Fulco di Verdura (FIG. 85).[16] The

85 (RIGHT) — Horst P. Horst, *Coco Chanel, Paris*, about 1937.

84 (BELOW) — Maison Gripoix for the House of Chanel, Maltese cross brooch, 1970s. Metal and glass.

86 — House of Chanel, bow necklace, 1983. Metal and glass.

87 (OPPOSITE) — House of Christian Dior, *Lily of the Valley*, 1950s. Metal and glass.

cross symbol later became the inspiration behind Chanel's baroque-style gem-and-pearl versions that, one hundred years after their initial design, remain part of the couture house's lexicon (FIG. 84).

Only once, in 1932—at the height of the Great Depression, and in an effort to revive the diamond business—did Chanel create jewelry using precious materials. Titled *Bijoux de diamants* (Diamond jewelry), the collection coincided with elements of heightened femininity in the couturier's clothing, including lace and bows.[17] *Bijoux de diamants* even included a platinum and diamond necklace in the shape of a bow. Years later, when Karl Lagerfeld took the helm of the fashion house in 1983, his meticulous research led him to copy the design using rhinestones for part of his debut collection as creative director (FIG. 86).[18]

Jewelry played a role in seasonal presentations at all Parisian couture houses. The superstitious Christian Dior's favorite flower was the lily of the valley, a flower associated with France's May Day festivities since the sixteenth century. For Dior, it was his own lucky charm. He embroidered the form on dresses,

BRILLIANCE

featured it as a key ingredient in Dior perfumes, and used it in jewelry designs. In one necklace, made in the 1950s, poured glass petals offer a dimensionality that mirrors the lily's leaves, and pearls form the flower's small white blossoms (FIG. 87). The necklace drapes around the neck to offer the wearer protection.

Over the decades that followed, couturiers continued to present jewelry in their fashion shows. As runway presentations grew increasingly choreographed, it became even more essential that the jewelry worn on stage have the ability to be read at a glance, as models quickly moved past rows of seated clients and journalists. At Lanvin, Elie Top designed jewelry under the helm of Alber Elbaz, who brought a sense of "imperfect perfection" to the century-old couture house.[19] In February 2013, when Lanvin presented their fall collection, five of Top's nameplate-inspired necklaces sent a highly visible message to audiences, the words "Cool," "Help," "Happy," "Hot," and "You" suspended from models' necks (FIG. 88).

Just as our perceptions of jewelry change when it is shown on runways or in fashion editorials, so too does our understanding shift when jewelry interacts with skin. Artists creating one-of-a-kind or limited-edition works also think about wearability as they design jewelry to be worn by collectors. In the United

88 — Elie Top for House of Lanvin, *You*, 2013. Metal, resin, glass, and silk.

89 — Peter Basch, model wearing Art Smith's *Modern Cuff*, about 1948.

States, the connection between jewelry and the body is perhaps best demonstrated in the work of Art Smith, an artist who intentionally left open areas of negative space in his work, allowing for the wearer's skin to become a key feature of the design. The Afro-Cuban artist was part of New York's mid-century studio jewelry movement, and was keenly aware of the way his jewelry would move in the world. Trained at Cooper Union, he first worked for jewelry artist Winifred Mason in Harlem before opening an eponymous shop on Cornelia Street in New York's Greenwich Village in 1946. His studio and shop pulsed with the rhythms of jazz music, and his work integrated aspects of Surrealism and biomorphic concepts, invoking organic and natural forms (FIG. 89).

Inspired by music and fashion, the artist's large-scale *Ellington* necklace is a lyrical showstopper (SEE FIG. 12). Undulating silver lines include open areas through which the wearer's chest, or bodice, would have been visible. The extraordinary ornament was prominently featured in the window of his shop, where it was seen and bought by Ruth Ellington, sister to the jazz legend for whom the necklace is named. According to Smith's partner, Charles Russell, *Ellington* didn't suit Ruth's stature or style, and she ultimately gave it to a friend: the pianist Don Shirley, whose life was dramatized in the 2018 film *Green Book*.[20] In 2008, when the Brooklyn Museum mounted a retrospective of Smith's jewelry, a version of his *Ellington* necklace appeared on a model in *Vogue*, allowing the work to be seen with an eye toward fashion and scale that is usually impossible in the museum setting.[21]

Beginning in the 1960s, fashion designers like Pierre Cardin offered jewelry on a similar scale to Smith's, introducing metal into fashion *and* fashion jewelry. Sometimes Cardin's jewelry-like elements were directly connected to his garments: a little black dress made around 1969 features a necklace-like breastplate falling down the front, exposing the wearer's skin between each chrome element. Other times, the jewelry was a separate entity (FIGS. 90–91). Although Cardin and his contemporaries created many outlandish pieces under the umbrella of the Space Age design movement, much of their work was highly wearable and perfectly paired with the era's streamlined mini dresses. The era saw a wave of new materials, designer names, and a growing bond between jewelry and fashion. The decade also witnessed Europe's introduction of high-end, ready-to-wear fashions, called prêt-à-porter, which offered customers the versatility of mixing and matching garments and accessories.

As Italian jewelry designer Elsa Peretti commented in 1982, "It's more fun to wear basic clothes and have lots of accessories."[22] Peretti, who introduced silver jewelry to a young, fashionable audience beginning in the late 1960s, is remembered best for her decades working for Tiffany & Co. In fact, many of the designs still retailed there today were first created by Peretti more than half a century

90 — Otto Bettmann, model wearing
Pierre Cardin design, 1969.

91 — Pierre Cardin, necklace, 1971.
Chrome and acrylic.

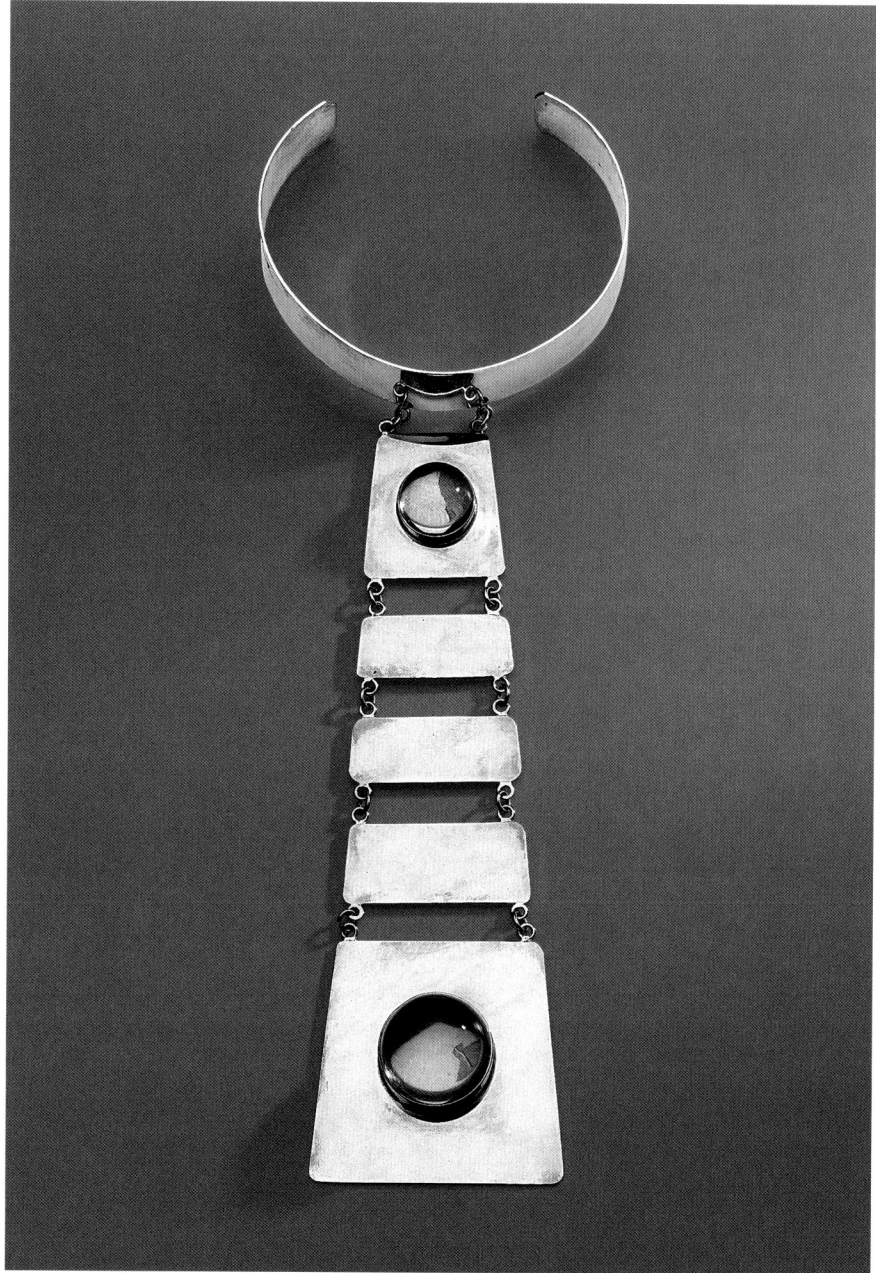

ago. After leaving Rome and settling in Barcelona, the designer moved to New York to explore a career in modeling. Almost immediately upon her arrival, she became part of the city's fashionable set, working with fashion designers Giorgio di Sant'Angelo and later Halston. She collaborated with Halston for years, exhibiting jewelry and accessories in his fashion shows even after joining Tiffany & Co. in 1974. A number of the fashion designer's famous clients helped to publicize the jeweler's work, including their friend Liza Minnelli, who wore

Halston clothing and Peretti jewelry when promoting her 1972 film *Cabaret* and, in 1973, accepting the Academy Award for Best Actress (FIG. 92).

One of Peretti's earliest designs was the now-iconic *Bone Cuff* (FIG. 93). As a child, she would visit the Santa Maria della Concezione dei Cappuccini in Rome with her nanny. The artist had a habit of slipping the elaborately decorated and patterned bones of Capuchin friars from the church's crypt into her pocket or purse—she liked the way they felt in her hand. Invariably, Peretti's mother would find the bones, reprimand her daughter, and send her to return them. That didn't stop the young designer, though; instead, it fueled her imagination for years to come. Later, as an adult living in Barcelona and the surrounding countryside, Peretti was reminded of the stolen bones during a visit

92 — Jack Mitchell, Liza Minnelli wearing *Medium Bone Cuff* by Elsa Peretti for Tiffany & Co., 1972.

93 — Elsa Peretti for Tiffany & Co., *Large Bone Cuff*, about 1978. Silver.

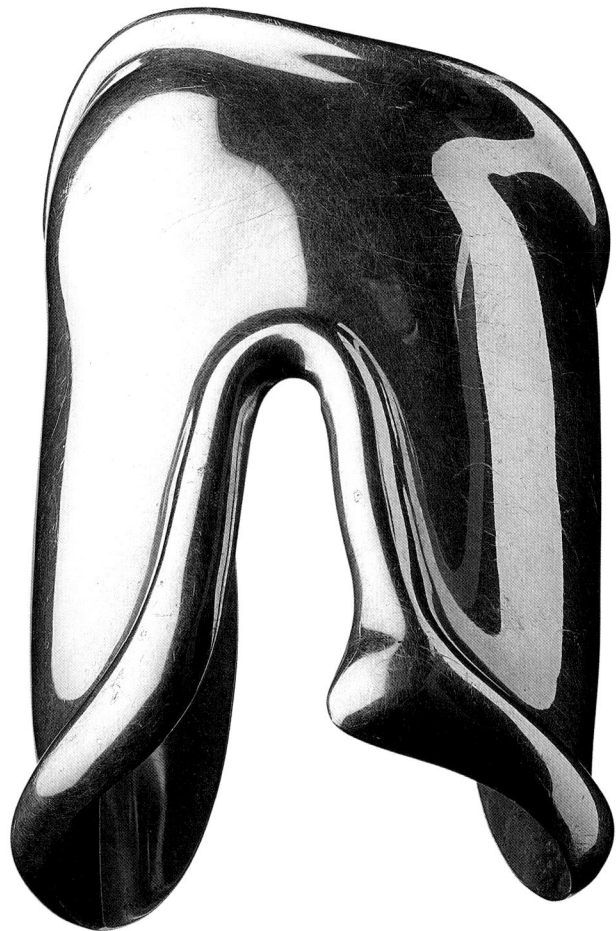

94 — Mallory Weston, *Python Hot Pants*, 2016. Gold-filled bronze, silver, copper, steel, leather, and cotton.

to Antoni Gaudí's Sagrada Familia cathedral. At Halston's suggestion, she designed a bone bracelet in small, medium, and large widths. The most substantial version includes a split in the middle, intended to evoke the space between the radius and ulna, the two bones spanning the wrist.

The size and scale of the *Large Bone Cuff*, when worn on the wrist, bring to mind a protective gauntlet, such as those worn by Wonder Woman. Gal Gadot, the actor who played the superhero in a 2017 film, wore the cuff on the cover of *Elle* magazine as a nod to Wonder Woman's costume. Still popular after nearly half a century, the iconic bracelet remains as sought after today as when it was first introduced in 1971. As Peretti described, "My love of bones has nothing macabre about it…Things that are forbidden remain with you forever."[23] The natural world was a central inspiration for the designer, who worked using a reductive process, taking something like a bone, horseshoe, or heart, omitting all unnecessary elements, and softening the edges, creating an abstracted version of the original.

Just as Peretti blurred the lines between jewelry and the body by transforming human bones into jewels, contemporary artists continue to push the boundaries between fashion and jewelry. While cutting and sewing may be more at home in a fashion studio than at a metalsmith's bench, artists such as Mallory Weston borrow materials and techniques from textiles. Weston, who teaches at Temple University's Tyler School of Art and Architecture in Philadelphia, cuts and sews metal elements into oversized hearts, bows, and smiley-face designs reminiscent of the colorful artwork that Lisa Frank popularized among adolescents during the 1980s and 1990s. Weston expanded on this work in 2016 with *Python Hot Pants*, which she presented at Pulse Miami Contemporary Art Fair. Hot pants originated in the 1960s and were made fashionable in the disco days of the 1970s, when fashion designers like Halston paired them with long coats. In a world that had only just come to terms with women in pants, these shortest-of-shorts were radical. After the actor Catherine Bach, star of the television series *Dukes of Hazzard*, wore short denim cut-offs, the style became popularly known as "Daisy Dukes," after her character. Decades after their acceptance into popular culture, Weston created her own pair of hot pants, custom-fitted to herself, that mirrors the look of snakeskin. Hand-cut gold, silver, copper, and steel elements sewn onto leather create a luminous garment that merges fashion and jewelry (FIG. 94). Both revealing and concealing the body, the pants are at once an object of fashion and contemporary jewelry.

Jewelry moves through the world on the body. Fundamental in creating a fashion statement or offering a sense of fantasy or whimsy, jewelry adds sparkle to the human canvas. From costume and fine jewelers to contemporary makers, artists expand on the art form, asking viewers—and wearers—to think about where fashion and the body end, and where jewelry begins. When displayed in museum collections, however, these objects lack the bodies they were created to adorn. The objects are, of course, still appreciated for their artistry and technical prowess, but much is gained by thinking about the collectors and wearers who animated these jewels through their history. On the gallery pages that follow, jewelry is illustrated alongside paintings, photographs, and sculptures to bring these works of art to life and aid in the imagination of them, not just as the "whatisit" that Art Smith described, but as the artists intended—on the body.

After Clarice Sebag-Montefiore married Alphonse de Rothschild on November 20, 1912, her new marital status entitled her to wear a tiara. The English-born baroness wore this spectacular jewel—which could also be styled as a necklace—to formal "white tie" events, as tradition dictated.

96 (OPPOSITE) — Evelyn Vanderhoop, *Raven's Tail*, 2017–18. Wool, sea otter fur, cedar bark fiber, shell, and copper thread.

97 — Tiffany Vanderhoop, *Naaxiin Ghost Face*, 2022. Brass and glass.

Evelyn Vanderhoop weaves by hand on Haida Gwaii in the Pacific Northwest. This intricate robe was designed for cultural ceremonies, where the long fringe comes alive to the rhythm of drum music. Her daughter Tiffany's long beaded earrings, made in the same color palette, move in a similar way when worn on the ears. Their design was inspired by Naaxiin (Chilkat) textile arts, as well as traditional Haida symbols and motifs.

98 (OPPOSITE) — Mariko Kusumoto, *Sea Creatures*, 2015. Polyester organza and monofilament.

This fantastical necklace by Mariko Kusumoto uses sculpted textiles and threads to encircle the body in a sea anemone. After fashion designer Jean Paul Gaultier encountered her work at the Museum of Modern Art, he asked her to collaborate for his Spring/Summer 2019 collection. In *Big in Japan*, Kusumoto adorned Gaultier's designs with wonderfully translucent purple, blue, and pink "brooches."

99 — Pascal Le Segretain, model Soo Joo Park wears the *Big in Japan* ensemble while walking for Jean Paul Gaultier at Paris Fashion Week, 2019.

100 (OPPOSITE) — G. Paulding Farnham, Renaissance Revival neck ornament, 1900–1904. Platinum, gold, enamel, diamond, ruby, emerald, cat's eye, chrysoberyl, sapphire, and pearl.

The inspiration for this turn-of-the-century chain came from Renaissance portraits of sitters wearing similar styles. In the sixteenth century, these jewels were likely sewn onto sitters' clothing. G. Paulding Farnham's interpretation of these ornaments, which would have been far less practical in the early twentieth century, showcases the dynamism of Tiffany & Co. artisans, and may have been exhibited at one of the era's many international expositions.

101 — Circle of Corneille de Lyon, *Françoise de Longwy*, about 1527.

102 — Necklace, Miao, 1920s. Silver.

This large torque was made by a Miao silversmith working in southwest China. A complete set of ceremonial jewels, which would include a necklace like this, can weigh up to twenty pounds, denoting wealth and status. This piece alone weighs nearly two pounds.

103 (OPPOSITE) — Bulgari, necklace, about 1986. Gold, pearl, tourmaline, citrine, and peridot.

Italian jewelry house Bulgari has long cultivated an international celebrity clientele that has included Hollywood actors—most famously Elizabeth Taylor—as well as European royalty. Bulgari's jewelry from the 1980s was a careful study of color: in combining hues from opposite ends of the color spectrum, their work complemented the period's bold fashions.

104 — Ear rods, Coclé, 700–1520.
Gold and greenstone.

These ear rods, made with two of the most precious materials in Mesoamerica, were Coclé symbols of rank and power. Figural art indicates that these ornaments were worn in pairs, and would have glimmered as their wearer moved or spoke, drawing attention to the face.

105 — Drinking vessel, Mayan, 650–850.
Earthenware and slip paint.

BRILLIANCE

106 (OPPOSITE) — Charles Robert Ashbee, marsh-bird brooch, 1901–02. Gold, silver, enamel, moonstone, topaz, and pearl.

This brooch by Charles Robert Ashbee was originally mounted to a tortoise-shell hair comb. Made by metalworker A. Gabhardt and enamelist William Mark in a small English workshop, the brooch's transparent plique-à-jour enamel would have been striking when worn in the stylish updos of the early twentieth century.

107 — merry renk, *Branching*, 1967. Silver and pearl.

merry renk, a primarily self-taught artist, was an instrumental player in the studio jewelry movement in the United States. Beginning in the late 1940s, renk experimented with jewelry, creating ornaments made from wire. This hair comb from the late sixties anticipates the renaissance such decorative objects enjoyed as long hair once again became fashionable.

The glamorous fashions of the 1920s and 1930s included stacks of glittering gem-set bracelets. With the introduction of costume jewelry, the styles worn on screen by movie stars and in fashion photographs became attainable for the average woman. Department stores in the United States retailed copies of fine jewelry, allowing women to stack bracelets made of rhinestones and less expensive metals to create a similar effect.

108 — Ann Ray, *Secret, interrupted*, 1998.

Trailblazing fashion designer Lee Alexander McQueen partnered with jeweler Shaun Leane to produce some of the turn of the century's most provocative runway presentations. This photograph was taken backstage as Leane's *Joan* headdress was assembled on a model's head. Shown as part of McQueen's *Joan of Arc* collection in Autumn/Winter 1998, the ornament blurs the lines between fashion, jewelry, and accessories.

BRILLIANCE

The introduction of the pomander coincided with the development of early modern cities. The luxury object was often designed to look like a small fruit that opened to reveal spice-filled wedges. Used to mask unpleasant scents or for medicinal purposes, pomanders were sometimes worn on the body for easy access.

BODY AS CANVAS

III — Frans Pourbus the Elder, *Portrait of a Woman*, 1581.

112 — John Thomson, *China: a Manchu lady having her face painted, Beijing*, 1869.

113 — Hairpin, Chinese, 19th century. Metal, kingfisher feather, jade, coral, colored gemstones, imitation pearl, and silk-wrapped wire.

Since the Han Dynasty (206 BC–220 AD), the bright blue feathers of the kingfisher bird have been prized in China for their color and iridescent quality. Used in jewelry and accessories, the feathers were often combined with dangling gemstones to create a captivating effect when worn on the body or pinned in the hair.

114 — Anna Hu, *Enchanted Ania*, 2023.
Titanium, spinel, and diamond.

Anna Hu's close examination of orchids,
a symbol of integrity and virtue, led her to
study art and poetry about the plant. This
life-size blossom brooch, modeled after
the rare *Ania hookeriana* and fabricated in
titanium, is a surprisingly lightweight
statement jewel.

ROTHSCHILD BROOCH AND NECKLACE-TIARA

VICTORIA REED WITH
BETTINA BURR AND EMILY STOEHRER

115 — Baron and Baroness Alphonse and Clarice de Rothschild with their children, Albert, Bettina, and Gwendoline, 1937.

On December 3, 1938, the German Reich's Nazi regime passed a law forbidding Jewish citizens from freely buying or selling anything made of gold, platinum, silver, or precious stones: luxury objects exactly like the tiara—which can also be worn as a necklace—and brooch which belonged to Clarice Rothschild of Vienna. Such items could only be taken to Nazi "purchasing agents" and sold for small amounts of money. This was one of many antisemitic laws that stripped Jewish residents of their financial and personal autonomy before the state nationalized and expropriated their property outright.

When Austria was annexed to the Third Reich in the Anschluss of March 13, 1938, laws that had already been passed by Nazi Germany— including those targeting Jews— were enforced in Austria right away.

Alphonse and Clarice Rothschild, members of a prominent banking family of Jewish descent, were immediately subject to Nazi persecution. The Rothschilds kept an extraordinary collection of fine art in their Vienna homes—some 3,500 paintings, sculptures, and pieces of decorative art, not to mention beautifully bound books. By 1939, just one year after the Anschluss, the Nazis had expropriated and inventoried the collection, which was later moved to a central depot. Adolf Hitler had the right of first refusal and selected many of the Rothschilds' works of art for his so-called Führermuseum, a project that was never realized. Other objects in the collection were taken for regional museums, and the books were handed over to the Austrian National Library. Portions of the jewelry, however, escaped Nazi depredation. At the time of the

Anschluss, Alphonse and Clarice were traveling in London, and Clarice had some of her finest jewelry with her. She never returned with it to Austria, and it remained in her possession.

After the end of World War II, Allied forces uncovered the caches of artwork the Nazis had put into storage. They set up collecting points to inventory looted works of art and other cultural objects, including those belonging to the Rothschilds, and ensured they were sent back to their countries of origin for restitution. By that time, the Rothschild family had relocated to the United States. Alphonse passed away in 1942, and by the end of the 1940s, most of the art collection was returned to Clarice. She had to apply to the postwar Austrian authorities, however, to have her collection shipped to the United States. In lieu of export fees,

117 — Necklace-tiara, European, about
1880. Silver, gold, pearl, and diamond.

118 — Philip de László, *Clarice de Rothschild*, 1925.

the government required her to "donate" 250 works of art to its state museums. These remained in Austria until they were returned to the family in the late 1990s.

Given these facts, it is all the more extraordinary that portions of the Rothschilds' jewelry collection survived. Many Jewish residents of Germany, Austria, and occupied Europe lost all of their jewels during the Holocaust. Some collections were looted, some were sold for subsistence, and some were forcibly surrendered to the Nazis in accordance with the law cited above.

Indeed, the jewels Clarice Rothschild left in Vienna remain untraced to this day. Unlike works of fine art, which were recovered on a large scale, jewelry was—and remains—widely dispersed. What accounts for the differences between the fate of fine art and jewelry? A painting, for example, can be attributed to a particular artist, described, and inventoried. Marks of ownership can be recorded on the backs and undersides of larger works of art, making them easier to trace. Paintings and sculptures are also more likely to be photographed,

exhibited, and even published. Jewelry, however, is kept in a domestic space; it is small, personal, and not always uniquely identifiable. How do you trace a diamond necklace once it has left your possession? How can you prove that it was yours? This is often a near impossible task; moreover, large amounts of jewelry containing gold, silver, and other precious materials would have been disassembled and sold in pieces during the war.

The necklace-tiara and brooch shown here are part of a larger group of thirteen pieces of jewelry which the descendants of Alphonse and Clarice Rothschild donated to the MFA in 2013 (FIGS. 116–17; SEE FIG. 95). They are testament to the strength and resilience of a family that survived one of the darkest periods in recent history.

A CONVERSATION BETWEEN BETTINA BURR, VICTORIA REED, AND EMILY STOEHRER

The Rothschild jewelry arrived at the MFA thanks to the generosity of the family's descendants, most notably Bettina "Nina" Burr, Alphonse and Clarice's granddaughter, and a Museum Trustee (SEE FIG. 115). Unlike other parts of the family's donation, which were looted during the Nazi era and later restituted, this jewelry remained in the family's possession. In a conversation with MFA curators, Burr reflected on what these pieces meant to her family, and how they relate to the family's extensive art collection.

EMILY STOEHRER: Can you tell us a little about this collection?

NINA BURR: What I'd always heard about the emerald brooch was that my grandfather gave it to my grandmother on the occasion of their wedding anniversary in 1937 (FIG. 116). And then, of course, I had to go see when they got married, and in the course of doing some of that, I came across a list in *The Times of London* from November 20, 1912, of the wedding gifts, primarily jewelry.

ES: Diamond tiara, diamond chain, diamond pendant, diamond combs. What an incredible find.

NB: And then, of course, I thought, *Is this the piece that I remember?* Louis and Eugène were my grandfather's brothers, and they gave [Clarice] a pearl rope with a diamond clasp. It may be the rope of pearls that's in the portrait by László (FIG. 118).

ES: From this article, your recollection, and the gift to the MFA, it's clear that your grandmother had an incredible jewelry collection.

NB: I think she took a lot of it with her to London [before the war]. What you have here is what I inherited from my mother. But my aunt— my mother's sister—also inherited jewelry from my grandmother.

VICTORIA REED: Why did she take her jewelry with her to London at that time?

NB: The former King of England, George V, had been a great stamp collector. My grandfather was also a huge stamp collector, and it was actually quite a small world at the top, so there was a fair amount of back and forth. What I always heard

was [Alphonse and Clarice] went to London for the opening of an exhibition of stamps. Because the visit was going to involve appearances with the new King of England, George VI, it was definitely a time to show what you had.

ES: So it would've been normal for her to bring a large amount of jewelry on such a trip?

NB: Oh, yeah. Trunks. It was a totally different lifestyle than what we are used to today. My grandmother held onto her jewelry. What happened was my grandfather had…not all of his stamp collection, because there were books and books of stamps that stayed in Vienna that were then taken, and I don't think they ever reappeared. But he had, still, an array of stamps, and it was from the sale of the stamps that my grandparents were able to exist during the time that they moved from Austria to Switzerland, and then to England and the US.

ES: Jewelry holds such a personal place in people's lives, and that they sold the stamps but kept the jewelry makes me think that it was very special to them.

NB: My grandmother was very forceful, and my grandfather was much more…what's the word? He was an intellectual, and his persona was really quite quiet and thoughtful, but he was not a big personality. In fact, he put himself in the background as much as he could, and he adored my grandmother. And anything that would've made her happy, he would've been 100% behind. Guess what?

VR: She wanted her jewelry?

NB: [Nods.] And actually, as it turned out, the stamps were incredibly valuable.

ES: Fascinating. When the MFA first exhibited your family's gift back in 2014, [the French jewelry house] Boucheron's archives reached out to me with a photograph of the diamond tiara-necklace (SEE FIG. 95). Although it's unmarked, they felt confident that they had made it for your family.

NB: I think so, because their tastes were conservative. They would've gone to the established jewelers versus reaching out to contemporary jewelers who made things that were more Jugendstil.

VR: The art collection is the same way.

NB: Exactly, Torie. The art collection is the same way. It's very conservative.

ES: What does this jewelry mean to you?

NB: For me, it's a reminder of a bygone era, of people I love very much, and of the wonders of these works of art. I've always thought they were simply beautiful. It's special. It brings back memories. Oh, it's a joy seeing those pieces on view at the MFA. It really is. It's so nice seeing people looking at them.

GOLDFINGER

BELLA NEYMAN

B runo Martinazzi's *Goldfinger* bracelet is a complicated object to write about, think about—even wear (FIG. 119). When I first encountered the piece at the home of a collector, I was eager to try it on. I am a firm believer that jewelry belongs on the body, and that the wearer and the maker are involved in a mutual relationship: the artist needs the wearer's body to be the messenger who carries forth their voice, and the wearer wants to be adorned by the artist's work, not simply for the sake of beauty, but as an expression of value, both financial and moral. I slipped on the bracelet, and, gripped by this gold, masculine hand—both metaphorically and physically—I thought about control, about the subjugation of women. After learning more about Martinazzi's life and work, I have since reconsidered this interpretation, coming to believe

that a work I once thought was about aggression is, rather, about reconciliation.

The Italian jeweler and sculptor was educated at the University of Turin as a chemist, and pursued an apprenticeship as a goldsmith with the Musa brothers. There, he created traditional jewelry in yellow gold and platinum, with semi-precious stones. By all accounts, Martinazzi was a humanitarian; his longtime friend, the gallerist and educator Helen Drutt, described him as a "pacifist."[1] As Carla Gallo Barbisio, a professor of psychology at the University of Turin, wrote, "Martinazzi firmly decline[d] any interest in any kind of violent expression in human nature, even in sports.... He condemn[ed] all war and bloodshed and searche[d] for a different possible dimension of the human being."[2] A deeply philosophical man, the jeweler was

affected by the social and political events taking place around him in the late 1960s, known in Italy as the Years of Lead, which were marked by student protests and political terrorism.

In response to this unrest, the nature of Martinazzi's work changed. He began to make work that was visually fragmented, never focusing on the body as whole, but rather on its parts—such as the mouth, navel, and buttocks—a displacement which he called "a symbol of societal living in superabundance eating itself up in a self-destructive insatiability."[3] In the early 1960s, Martinazzi began making large-scale stone sculptures of body parts detached from the whole. He placed these artworks in fields or gardens, and the experience of encountering them is not unlike that of coming across a piece of jewelry in an urban setting. Confronted by the burden of isolation, Martinazzi's sculptures ask the viewer to consider their existence— the parts that make up the whole.

In 1969, the same day an exhibition of Martinazzi's work was set to open in Milan, a terrorist deployed a bomb in the city's Piazza Fontana. This event deeply shook the artist; that same year, he created *Goldfinger*. The bracelet, part of an edition of twenty-four—twelve of a man's left hand and twelve of his right hand— is designed in such a way that the fingers wrap around the top of the wearer's wrist, with the thumb placed underneath. In effect, the jewelry's positioning is that of a hand grasping another, a powerful statement when you consider that, most often, the hand the man is taking hold of belongs to a woman.

133

119 — Bruno Martinazzi, *Goldfinger,*
1969. Gold.

Drutt, however, believes that Martinazzi chose to show beauty in place of suffering. She has said that *Goldfinger*, which was part of her personal collection, did not stir up negative emotions in her, but instead brought her "great comfort, close around [her] wrist."[4] It is true that Martinazzi used his art to temper the ugliness of the violence that surrounded him, imbuing work fraught with political meaning with beauty and optimism. In 1967, he made two pieces, a bracelet and a brooch, both titled *Marce della Pace,* or march for peace. Each depicts a group of abstracted figures, the closeness of their bodies suggesting a call to action. Later, in 1972, he was invited by Umberto and Gianni Agnelli to create a sculpture for the Fiat management headquarters in Turin. Martinazzi created two large fists, a monument to the working force inside the factories as well as "a symbol of creativity and tool of inventive spirit of knowledge."[5] Completed in 1978, the fists serve as a call to resistance.

When an opportunity presented itself to exhibit the sculpture at the Venice Biennale in 1980, Martinazzi declined the invitation, worried that the political situation of the time was too volatile for the work to have a global audience. This episode, combined with general ongoing unrest, left the artist depressed and forced him into a long period of isolation outside Turin.[6] Drutt first met Martinazzi during this period, at the World Crafts Council in 1980. An important collector in her own right, she went on to represent the jeweler through her eponymous Philadelphia gallery, acquiring

many of his pieces—including *Goldfinger*—for her own collection along the way. It is through Drutt's gallery that the piece was acquired by prominent art collector and philanthropist Daphne Farago, who gifted it to the MFA Boston in 2006.

I have long thought that the title of the bracelet, *Goldfinger*, was a nod to the 1964 James Bond film—and villain—of the same name, where a key character is declared dead from "skin suffocation" after her body is found covered in gold paint. I now believe that Martinazzi saw gold as a substantive material: there is an inner truth, a reality, in gold. When life becomes too difficult to accept, we must go back to the basics in search of answers. As Martinazzi remarked in 1989:

This diffuse dimension is what you feel when you experience the painful sensation that knowledge is possible only by splitting up the universe into small parts, the necessity of the fragmentation of the whole....And the instrument of knowledge and their images come into play: mouth, hands, eyes, feet....I want to tell the experience of knowledge and the anxious state of mind that I feel when the two things are near: the chaos of sentiments and the order of concepts.

The *Goldfinger* bracelet, then, does not wrest control from women and symbolize their subjugation, but rather alerts us to the notion that, as a society, we are broken.

WE TWO

JOYCE J. SCOTT

I believe I am the only person who Arthur Smith ever collaborated with. We met at Haystack Mountain School of Crafts in 1974. After I graduated in 1970 from the Maryland Institute College of Art, when I was twenty-one, and later attending graduate school in Mexico, I was twenty-four or twenty-five. He'd look at my work and say, "I don't know what you're doing—just don't stop." There, we began a long and wonderful relationship where we were not only friends, but mentor and mentee. I, of course, was the mentee.

The necklace we collaborated on is one of the pieces that Art repeated in a variety of materials—maybe silver, copper, and bronze. One day, we talked about working together. He didn't do that with other people, but because he liked the way I manipulated beads (and because I was a rascal and I probably bugged him), we decided to make a piece

together (FIG. 121). It's very different from his other jewelry, because he didn't normally integrate other materials like this. I had to figure out—with Art's help—how to integrate beadwork into the necklace in a way that was easy to wear and aesthetically beautiful, as well as made sense for the collaboration.

He made his piece first, called the *Half and Half* necklace, and then I added the beads. We decided to use this particular design because it had components that I could add to and rework. I wrapped beads around the existing coils, and he cut out a shape for me to mimic in beadwork, which we then mounted just as if he were mounting a stone, except using sewing instead of soldering.

One of the things I enjoy most about Art's work is that it is made to be worn. *Half and Half* has a velocity to it. It's rhythmic, and it fits around the neck in a really cozy

way (FIG. 120). It fits on different sized necks because of the way it's constructed. You can make it symmetrical, or move it to one side. It's like a dancer on your neck.

As an African American visual and performing artist who has attended many residencies and classes, it was wonderful for me to learn from an artist of such esteem—such great skill—who was also Black, and an Icon. I was young, and eager to learn from such a master. Art was well known, and his work had been worn by models and performers around the world. That was very tasty to me. He turned out to be quite the mentor—a very giving godfather.

Sometimes people ask me, "Do you have a favorite part, component, or moment in this piece?" I think one of the real strengths of *We Two* is that in this collaboration, Art's metal and my beads work equally. They caress each other equally.

120 (OPPOSITE) — John Dean, Joyce J.
Scott wearing *We Two*, about 1993–96.

121 — Joyce J. Scott and Art Smith,
We Two, after 1974. Brass, glass,
and leather.

STATEMENT
JEWELS

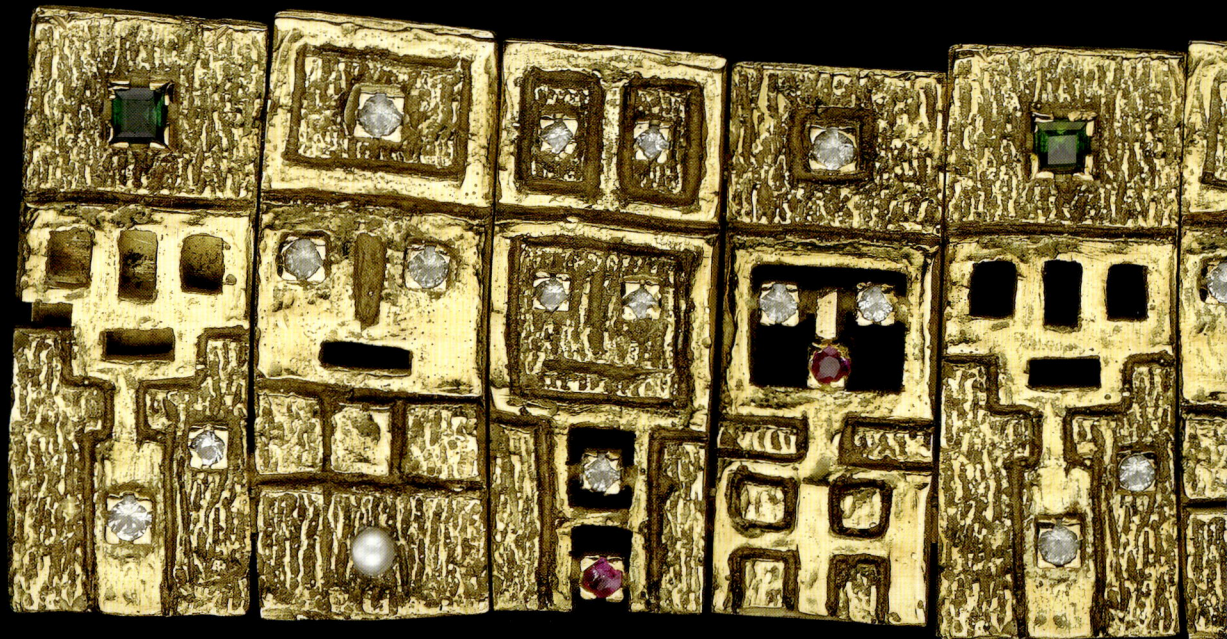

122 — Raphael Kirchner, woman smoking on a bicycle, 1900.

J ewelry speaks volumes. Whether serving as emblems of national pride or symbols of personal identity, jewelry—like fashion—is often used to make a statement. Because of its highly visible nature, jewelry offers a way to express both one's aesthetic tastes and personal beliefs publicly, on the body. This is as true today as it was hundreds of years ago. People communicate their status, sexual availability, politics, grief, belonging, and so much more in the jewelry they wear.

Take one small gold and diamond bicycle brooch: it may be a surprising symbol of feminism, but the bike changed the way women moved in the world (FIG. 122). Made by the English firm Streeter & Co. Ltd. in the 1890s, the brooch is a miniaturized version of the bicycle known as a diamond-frame machine. Like its inspiration, the gem features twisting handlebars, movable wheels with brilliant-cut diamonds—perhaps a playful nod to the bicycle's name—and pedals that spin when manipulated. The creation of this brooch coincided with a cycling craze that swept through Great Britain, Europe, and the United States at the height of the women's suffrage movement, the bike becoming a symbol of female independence.

During this period—and even today—bikes were gendered in their design and marketing. Men's bikes have a high crossbar that one has to step up and over, whereas women's bikes feature a dropped crossbar designed to accommodate the long skirts of the past. At first glance, Streeter & Co.'s brooch might appear to be made for a man; however, the diamond-frame bicycle it is based on was designed specifically for women in rational cycling dress (FIG. 123). Offering safety and comfort, these costumes included some of the earliest pants designed for women. Although the pants were quite voluminous and were sometimes referred to as a bifurcated skirt, the garment still allowed for an important freedom of movement. This is a brooch that was designed for a woman who was at the "cutting edge of female cycling fashion," had considerable wealth, and chose to make a statement about the newfound freedoms the bicycle offered.[2]

As part of a language of signs, jewelry carries power and meaning. It can be embedded with personal stories, or send messages that are instantly recognizable to a particular group or culture. Because of its highly visible nature, jewelry offers a way to wear one's "heart on their sleeve"—or around the wrist, on a backpack, lapel, or anywhere one chooses—as a powerful signifier of aesthetic tastes and personal beliefs. Jewelry can communicate one's identity, heritage, or even values. It can convey national or cultural pride, or express sociopolitical leanings. Operating like a secret language, these physical messages hold intimate meaning to their wearers.

In the eighteenth century, as groups organized in Britain and the United States to abolish the transatlantic slave trade, a designer working for the

BRILLIANCE

124 — Wedgwood Manufactory,
Am I Not a Man and a Brother?, 1786–87.
Jasperware and gold.

Englishman Josiah Wedgwood borrowed from classical iconography for his design of a ceramic "cameo" for the British Society for the Abolition of the Slave Trade.[3] The oval medallion designed by Henry Webber and modeled by William Hackwood for Wedgwood features a manacled enslaved man on bended knee with his arms raised under the question "Am I not a man and a brother?" (FIG. 124). The medallion was mass-produced and distributed to society members, who had them set into women's jewelry and men's accessories such as watch fobs or snuffboxes—highly visible indicators of support for the abolitionist movement. Like so much jewelry, it was intended as a conversation starter. The medallions reached American audiences in February 1788, when Wedgwood sent five hundred cameos along with a letter to Benjamin Franklin—then president of the Pennsylvania Abolition Society—expressing his "hope for the final completion of our wishes" to end the transatlantic slave trade.[4]

Wedgwood's highly successful medallion became a symbol of the abolitionist movement, and the central image and embedded phrase were featured prominently in other decorative arts and in graphic design. However, the line "Am I not a man and a brother?" did not capture the nuances of the abolitionist movement: while both the British and American organizations sought to end the slave trade, they were not advocating to end the practice of slavery entirely. Still, more than two hundred years later, Wedgwood's medallion remains an icon of the larger antislavery movement. The design speaks to the communicative nature of jewelry—and to how symbols can be misread.

A perhaps more straightforward political message is the wearing of one's national flag. Visible on the lapels of politicians during election cycles in the United States, the small, inexpensive pins are symbolic of a candidate's commitment to American ideals and patriotism. Over the course of US history, such brooches have been produced in a wide array of sizes and in everything from base metals and enamel to precious gems. A platinum, diamond, ruby, and sapphire Black, Starr & Frost flag brooch, commissioned by textile manufacturer Frederick C. Fletcher during World War I with plans to donate it to a charity auction, was intended to raise money for the war effort (FIG. 125). By the time the glitzy brooch was finished, however, the war was over.

In subsequent decades, jewelry continued to be used as a badge of self-expression. In 1941, designer Lester Gaba created the *Emblem of the Americas* brooch for the costume jewelry firm Coro (FIG. 126). The gold-plated brooch features the twenty-one flags of the Union of American Republics, with the United States in the center. The flagpoles are wrapped in a white banner which reads "Amigos Siempre" (Friends forever). The popular magazine *Ladies' Home Journal* promoted the design, and profits from the sale of the $3.95

125 — Black, Starr & Frost, flag brooch, 1917. Platinum, diamond, ruby, and sapphire.

126 — Lester Gaba for Coro, *Emblem of the Americas*, 1941. Gold-plated metal and epoxy.

127 — Eli Weinberg, Nelson Mandela wearing traditional beads during his time in hiding from the police, South Africa, 1961.

128 — Timothy Greenfield-Sanders, portrait of Secretary Albright as reproduced on the cover of Helen W. Drutt English's 1998 book *Brooching It Diplomatically: A Tribute to Madeleine K. Albright*, 2005.

brooch supported the Interamerican Scholarship Fund, which promoted student exchanges between American countries.[5] In support of the initiative, First Lady Eleanor Roosevelt wore the brooch in 1942.

During World War II, jewelry could demonstrate support for the Allied Forces. Experiencing a shortage of glass beads imported from Austria and Czechoslovakia—and cut off from the creative inspiration of Paris—jewelry designers in the United States adopted new styles. Patriotic brooches with American flags, military insignia, eagles, and Wings of Victory emblems became visible indicators of support for the war effort; they also added a pop of color to drab wartime clothing ensembles. While metal alloys including copper, tin, zinc, and nickel were used in these designs until 1941, after the US officially entered the war on December 7, 1941, the use of base metals was prohibited as they were needed for munitions manufacturing.[6] Gold plating replaced rhodium plating, and costume jewelers shifted to work in approved metals like lead and sterling silver until the end of 1947.

The practice of expressing one's politics through jewelry was not unique to those seeking to make a statement in the United States. The *ingqosha*, for example, is an iconic Xhosa beadwork collar from South Africa (FIG. 129). These necklaces are composed of thousands of glass seed beads threaded and woven together to form a flat necklace. Historically, Xhosa beadwork was worn by both men and women as a marker of social roles, status, or ethnic identity.[7] In the early twentieth century, Xhosa men wore collars and other beaded pieces for ceremonial occasions. In 1962, when anti-apartheid activist Nelson Mandela arrived at South Africa's Supreme Court to be sentenced on charges of treason against the apartheid government, he wore traditional Xhosa attire, including a beadwork collar (FIG. 127). By appearing in court in jewelry associated with the country's precolonial past, Mandela declared himself an Indigenous South African, questioned the nature of a Black African being judged by a white court, and protested the legitimacy of the trial.[8]

In taking action in this way, Mandela joined the long tradition of jewelry as a political tool. More recently, in the 1990s, US Secretary of State Madeleine Albright described how, after Saddam Hussein called her a serpent, she wore a snake pin to her next meeting with Iraqi officials. A decade later, in a *Newsweek* interview, she reminisced, "I thought, well, this is fun, so I went and I bought a lot of costume jewelry to kind of fit whatever the issue was we were going to be working on. When people would say, 'What are we going to do today?' or 'How do you feel?,' I said, 'Read my pins'" (FIG. 128).[9] With its long-standing association with wealth, jewelry has often functioned as a status symbol, but Albright's embrace of creative expression using inexpensive pins reminded many of jewelry's powerful and symbolic nature (SEE FIG. 165).

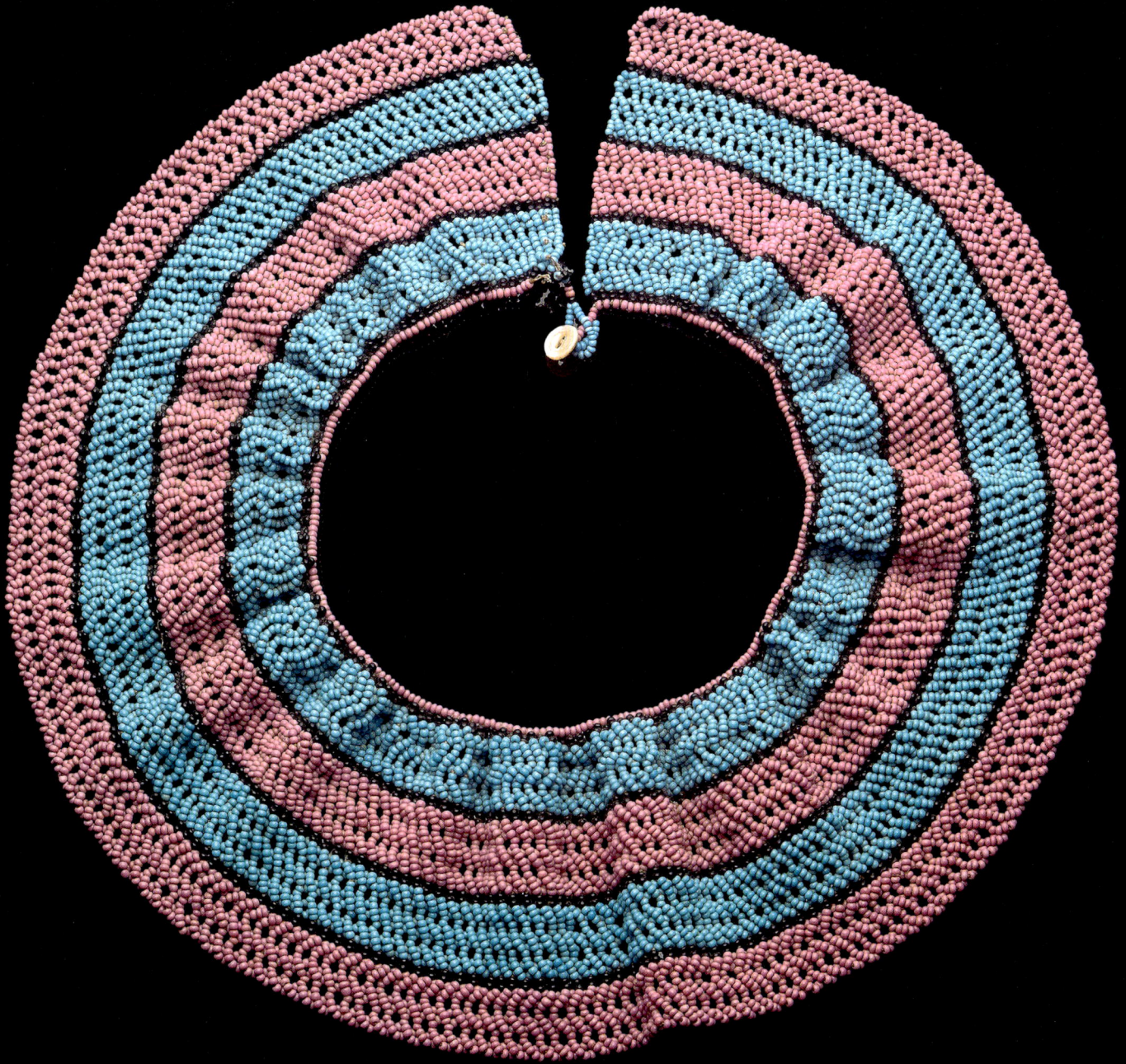

130 — Bracelet with image of Hathor, Nubian, 250–100 BC. Gold and enamel.

The practice of using jewelry to send a message extends beyond politics to express ideas like one's religious identity. Whether featuring gods and goddesses or connected to religious practices, for thousands of years, jewelry has carried spiritual power by communicating an association with the divine or speaking more symbolically to one's status within a religious group.

A gold bracelet featuring the Egyptian and Nubian goddess Hathor, a beloved and oft-represented female deity who protected women, is one of the earliest and most spectacular surviving examples of enamel jewelry (FIG. 130). Like with so many Egyptian jewels, the wearing of an image of Hathor was thought to have provided a "talismanic effect" that would protect the wearer in life and on their journey into the afterlife (SEE FIG. 67).[10] The goddess is featured on the bracelet's central panel of three hinged segments, all decorated with gold appliqués and blue, green, and red enamel. These color choices were highly symbolic: blue represented the life-giving waters of the Nile River; green was associated with vegetation and emblematic of renewal; and red evoked the color of blood and fire, and indicated power and vitality. The use of red enamel, which was difficult to produce and therefore rare, aided scholars in identifying the bracelet as a product of the Nubian city of Merōe, which boosted a "sophisticated glass industry" where "makers experimented with glass formulas and enamels."[11]

Egyptian cultures were not alone in using jewelry to seek spiritual protection, express religious beliefs, and connect wearers to the power of the divine. An outstanding Hindu pendant from the early eighteenth century, for example, depicts the ten incarnations of the god Vishnu (FIG. 131). However, the elaborate enamel narrative is meant to be hidden. It appears on the backside of the gem-set pendant, and would have been positioned close to the heart, either directly against the skin or resting on a garment. The front side of the jewel, which would have been the public, outward-facing side, features a large yellow sapphire surrounded by diamonds, emeralds, and rubies, keeping its religious nature private. Using transparent and opaque champlevé enamel, the artist filled the reverse side's center plaque and surrounding area with scenes depicting ten avatars of the Hindu god. An important divinity and a protector of law and order, Vishnu appears throughout Hindu iconography in many forms. Here, starting from the top left and moving clockwise around the pendant, the blue-skinned god is shown in various incarnations, as outlined in the sacred Hindu text the Bhagavata Purana.

While this pendant's scene is hidden, in other religions, the visibility of a jewel's message is a key component of its design. In Judaism, a synagogue will sometimes share a symbolic wedding ring with community members to wear as part of a marriage ceremony. Although there was originally no requirement for a ring to be used in Jewish weddings, in the medieval period, rings became a customary part of the ceremony. While more traditional Jewish wedding rings are simple bands, preferably in gold, without decorations and gemstones, more elaborate rings like the one in the MFA's collection—featuring a small

131 — Pendant depicting the ten incarnations of Vishnu, Indian, early 18th century. Gold, sapphire, diamond, emerald, ruby, and enamel. Left to right: front and back.

BRILLIANCE

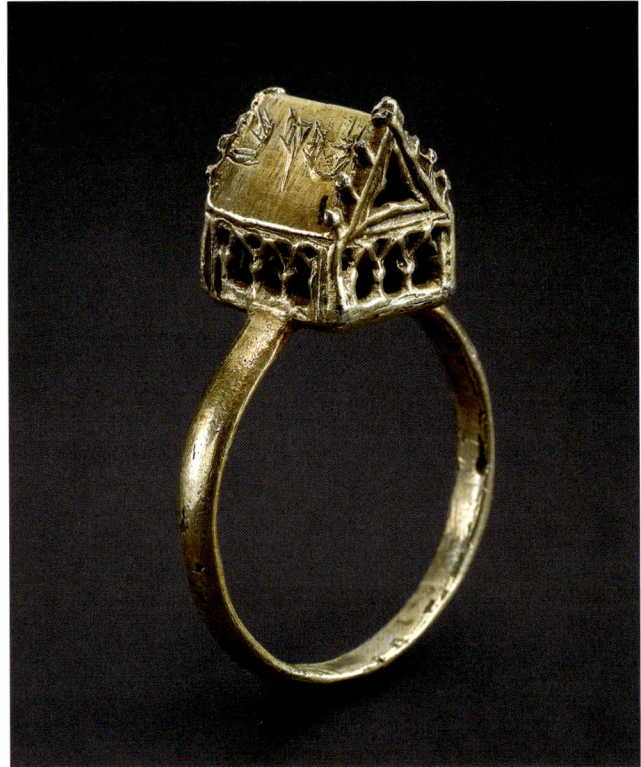

132 (LEFT) — Jewish wedding ring, Central European, 19th century. Gold and enamel.

133 (RIGHT) — Jewish engagement or wedding ring, German, found in Weissenfels, early 14th century. Gold-plated silver.

architectural form at the top symbolizing the Temple of Jerusalem—are believed by some to have been kept by the synagogue and shared by community members, to be worn only on the day of the marriage (FIG. 132). The jeweler who made this elaborate gold and enamel ring was likely influenced by two sources: first, the discovery of the Weissenfels Treasure in Germany in 1826 and the Colmar Treasure in France in 1863, each of which included similarly shaped rings dating from about 1300; second, the period's fashionable Renaissance Revival styles, which often incorporated polychrome enamel (FIG. 133; SEE FIG. 100). The scale of the architectural rings allowed witnesses of a ceremony to see the ring even from a distance, thereby validating the marriage.[12]

More than celebrating specific occasions in one's life, jewelry can also honor lifelong—or mundane—experiences and emotions. When made of certain materials, like hair or jet—a type of black fossilized wood that can be polished to a high shine—jewelry can function as a visual indicator of grief. It can also celebrate life, from ornaments evoking routine everyday experiences expressed visually to jewelry designed to honor lives lost.

Jewelry has a particularly close association with death. In one eighteenth-century example crafted from ivory, gold, glass, and human hair, a grieving mother, Ruth McConnell of Huntingdon, Pennsylvania, is depicted next to two urns, each representing a child who died (FIG. 134). McConnell gestures upward, toward two angels, as she stands under a symbolic weeping willow tree. The reverse of the jewel is inscribed, "In Memory of T. R. McC. Aged six years & three months and W. H. McC. aged 2 years & 10 months." Other markings note the maker, Parry & Musgrave, as well as the hair worker, J. Boone. Hair is one of the most intimate materials used in jewelry, and the lock included here was likely taken from the mother and both children, allowing the three to be linked after death, and for the mother to hold a piece of her children close to her body. Its deep symbolism clearly evident in its design, it would have been obvious to anyone who came in contact with the wearer that it was an object of mourning.

There is a long tradition of jewelry worn as part of mourning rituals, especially in nineteenth-century Europe and the United States. The associated jewels are mostly black, and are strongly connected to the concept of death as an ending. After First Lady Mary Todd Lincoln's son, William "Willie" Wallace, died of typhoid fever during the middle of the Civil War, she entered a long period of mourning. As she was an avid shopper with an eye for style, it is likely that Mary—during an 1864 spending spree—bought her black enamel and diamond brooch and matching earrings at Galt and Brothers in Washington, DC

134 — Rowland Parry, James Musgrave, and Jeremiah Boone, mourning pendant-brooch, 1792. Gold, watercolor on ivory, hair, and glass. Left to right: front and back.

135 — Brooch (left) with matching earrings (right), worn by Mary Todd Lincoln, about 1860. Gold, enamel, and diamond.

STATEMENT JEWELS

(FIG. 135).[13] As the nineteenth century had strict guidelines around the mourning period, including on what to wear throughout, this matching set would have been appropriate for the first lady to wear during the final stages of mourning, two years after the death of her son.

Following President Lincoln's assassination on April 15, 1885, Mary began the mourning process again—deeming this late-stage jewelry inappropriate—as she was simultaneously faced with moving out of the White House, finding a new home, and repaying $6,000 of debt.[14] Without income, she was forced to sell many of her possessions, including her matching brooch and earrings. An article on the sale appeared in *Frank Leslie's Illustrated Newspaper* on October 26, 1867, and included a drawing of the gems in their original box (FIG. 136). The article listed the suite's sale price as $350—likely the same price the First Lady had bought it for just a few years earlier. This sparked outrage in the media, as mounting such a sale was viewed as "sordid" and "disgraceful."[15] In light of the negative attention, many items failed to sell or sold for less than expected, and the sale did not raise the money she needed. As the first widow of an assassinated president, Lincoln petitioned Congress for a widow's pension—something she was not guaranteed upon the death of her husband. She asked to be paid the same amount as Civil War widows; eventually, in July 1870, she was awarded an annual pension of $3,000. The following year, her youngest son, Tad, died, and a few years later, in 1875, her only surviving son, Robert, committed Lincoln to a private sanitarium. The jewelry and objects connected to the First Lady's life are a testament to her place as a misunderstood and tragic figure in American history.

While nineteenth-century mourning jewelry focused on the loss of life and the suffering of those left behind, many other monumental jewels pay homage to a life well-lived. One such object of remembrance, or token of love and affection, is a simple gold bangle bracelet with an orb charm (FIG. 137). The gold ball opens, the interior spinning to cycle through the plaited hair of four family members: father, mother, George, and Robert. The bracelet, inscribed "RCB to HMW, 1864," was perhaps less an object of mourning than one of memory. Indeed, the sentiment of this bracelet is hidden and highly personal, and existed solely for the wearer, not the viewer. An 1866 British portrait of Lady Grace Charlotte Rose features a similar necklace (FIG. 138). Does it hold a secret element, too?

Jewels made to celebrate and remember a life are not confined to historical eras, but rather continue to be worn and crafted today. *Enuh*, a sculptural bracelet by contemporary Indigenous artist Lyndon Tsosie, centers a stylized figure created from opal inlaid with gold, and combines purple, blue, and red stones in an arrangement that brings to mind the colors, landscape, and sacred

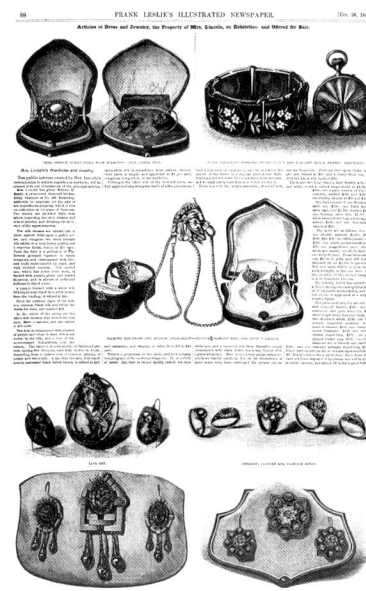

136 — Pages from *Frank Leslie's Illustrated Newspaper* advertising sale of Mary Todd Lincoln's wardrobe and jewelry, 1867.

137 — Bracelet, North American or European, 1864. Gold, glass, and hair.

138 — Frederick Sandys, *Grace Charlotte Rose (née Snow), Lady Rose*, 1866.

mountains of Navajo Nation, with its rolling hills and mesas.[16] The bracelet, whose title the artist translates as "life," was made shortly after the death of his father in 2017 (FIG. 139). Tsosie describes the central figure as representing "life, beauty, human beings, the soul—the beauty of human motherhood, fatherhood, childhood."[17] The head, half opal and half coral, represents the circle of life, the movement from day to night, and the passing of knowledge from one generation to the next.[18] Stressing its spiritual nature, Tsosie says, "Beauty is like God."[19] The connection to past, present, and future evident here also comes through in the work of many other Diné (Navajo) artists. Jewelry makes visible "culture and community—they are abstract and shared ideas made into concrete things."[20]

Jewelry is indeed a powerful vehicle for storytelling. It conjures thoughts of the moments in which it was given—and of the person who gave it—and allows the wearer to hold their memories close. Some jewelry artists, too, embrace a more narrative approach to the telling of stories. This style of creating grew in popularity in the late twentieth century, with artists narrating their ideas through their choices of subjects and materials; however, it built on a long tradition of designers telling a story through jewelry.

139 — Lyndon Tsosie, *Enuh* (Life), 2008.
Silver, gold, sugilite, lapis lazuli, spiny
oyster, and boulder opal.

BRILLIANCE

When England's Queen Victoria married Prince Albert of Saxe-Coburg Gotha on February 10, 1840, jewelry played an important role in the festivities (FIG. 140). In addition to exchanging rings with Albert during the ceremony, Victoria presented each of her twelve train bearers with a gift before the group returned to Buckingham Palace for the reception: a brooch designed by the prince and fabricated by Charles Augustus di Vé (FIG. 141).[21] While royal bridesmaids typically received a gift, usually a small brooch, the personal nature of this particular design broke with tradition. While each jewel was slightly different, all featured an eagle—perhaps taken from the Coburg coat of arms—set with a turquoise body, outstretched wings, a diamond beak, and round ruby eyes, pearls grasped tightly in its talons.[22] The chosen materials were laced with symbolism: blue turquoise to evoke the color of forget-me-nots, rubies to symbolize passion, diamonds to represent eternity, and pearls to denote true love. Nearly two hundred years later, these brooches remain a symbol of the couple's relationship.

142 (OPPOSITE) — François Boucher, *Pompadour at Her Toilette*, 1750, with later additions.

143 — Mrs. Philip (Charlotte) Newman and Georges Bissinger, necklace with a cameo of Elizabeth I, about 1890. Gold, silver, diamond, emerald, pearl, agate, and glass.

Queen Victoria's reign from 1819 to 1901 coincided with a wave of nationalism that swept through the United Kingdom and Europe. In both long-established and newly independent countries, jewelers sought to evoke the past in ornaments that expressed artistic, as well as political, meanings. A cameo necklace made around 1890, near the end of the Victorian Era, portrays the late Queen Elizabeth I, who reigned over England and Ireland from 1533 to 1603, in a nod to contemporary associations between the two powerful female monarchs (FIG. 143). This theme of feminine power extends to the necklace's creation: it was designed by Charlotte Newman, one of the earliest women to work in London as an independent jeweler. Known during her lifetime as Mrs. Newman or Mrs. Philip Newman, the artist trained in the city before opening her own workshop in the 1880s; unfortunately, surviving examples of her work are rare. For this pendant, Newman collaborated with celebrated French lapidary artist Georges Bissinger, who carved the central cameo of Elizabeth I.

144–145 — Melanie Bilenker, *Shaving (Viewfinder)*, 2017. Hair on paper, mineral crystal, mother-of-pearl, gold, and silver. Left to right: necklace and image seen from viewfinder.

The design for the surround that frames the cameo bears an uncanny resemblance to the clasp of a bracelet worn by Madame de Pompadour in a 1750 portrait by François Boucher (FIG. 142).[23] The painting shows de Pompadour, the mistress to King Louis XV of France, sitting at her toilette. In the midst of applying makeup, she stares out at the viewer. Her arm is bent; on her wrist, she wears a multistrand pearl bracelet with a sardonyx cameo of Louis XV set in a carved emerald and diamond frame—the same combination of gemstones Newman used in her image of Queen Elizabeth I. More than a passive consumer of fashion, Madame de Pompadour understood the communicative power of an ensemble: she was a patron of the arts and a collector of many things, including carved gems.[24] In featuring the bracelet so prominently, the painting makes clear the sitter's association with the king.

Made more than one hundred years apart, both cameos were fabricated by renowned Parisian carvers: Jacques Guay carved Louis XV in the eighteenth century, and Georges Bissinger carved Elizabeth I in the nineteenth. It is unclear whether or not Newman had seen the original cameo, as the painting was in private hands when the necklace was made, and later sold at auction in 1875. However, Pompadour's cameo survives and today is part of the National Library of France in Paris; the portrait hangs on the wall of the Harvard Art Museum in Cambridge, Massachusetts.[25]

Jewelry has the power to tell stories across eras and nations, big and small: tales of gods, countries, and kings, and of anniversaries, births, and deaths. It

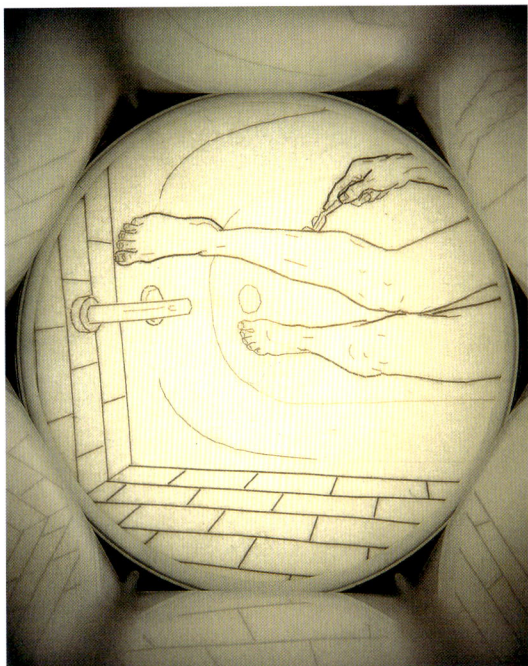

can be used to send messages between individuals, across a room, or through time. For contemporary Philadelphia-based artist Melanie Bilenker, even the most personal—and perhaps even mundane—stories can speak to the busy everyday lives of many twenty-first-century women. Inspired by Victorian hairwork jewelry, which typically featured hair that had been given to artists to plait on commission, Bilenker uses her own hair to illustrate moments in her life. In *Shaving*, designed to be worn as a pendant, a mother-of-pearl viewfinder reveals an image resembling a line drawing (FIG. 144). The dark outline, which looks like ink but is actually made of the Bilenker's hair, depicts the artist's hand holding a razor, shaving her legs in the bathtub (FIG. 145). Other examples of Bilenker's hairwork jewelry illustrate her cooking dinner, taking a nap, and gardening—scenes that are both incredibly personal and profoundly relatable.

People love hearing the stories of jewelry. At a gathering of jewelry enthusiasts, it's not uncommon to hear someone say, "Tell me about your necklace," or "What's the story behind that ring?" These sorts of questions usually lead to the wearer taking off the jewel and passing it around the table while telling of its creation and their connection to it: who made it, where they got it, and why it's special. These intimate encounters also happen in everyday life, among people whose time and work are less focused on jewelry, such as when someone has received a special gift or is showing off a new diamond engagement ring. A brooch or necklace might communicate one's political leanings; a ring, a recent marriage; a pendant, a recently deceased loved one. The narratives of jewelry transport both wearer and observer to important milestones, to a place or time, or to a culture we hold close.

Designed for independent women like herself, Elsa Peretti's *Scorpion* necklace features pincers that encircle the neck, as well as a venomous stinger intended to nestle between the wearer's breasts. The idea emerged from Peretti's observation of the feared—and respected—creatures in Sant Martí Vell, a Spanish village close to her heart.

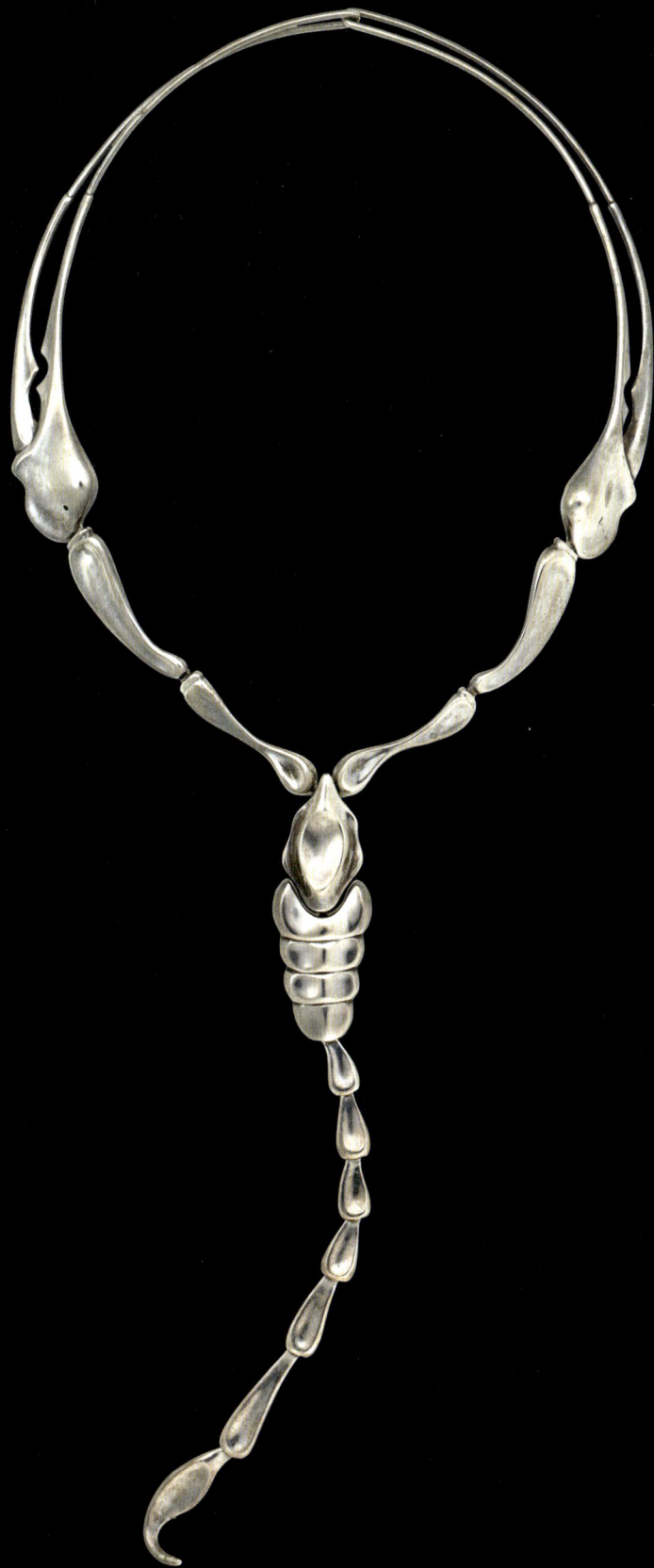

147 (OPPOSITE) — Tiffany & Co., Colt family necklace (left) and earrings (right), 1856. Gold, enamel, and diamond.

This set was given as a wedding present from gun manufacturer Samuel Colt to his bride, Elizabeth Jarvis, on June 5, 1856. Retailed by Tiffany and Co., it is one of the earliest surviving diamond jewels to bear the company's mark. In 1862, the *Hartford Daily News* reported that Mrs. Colt wore this necklace to the coronation of Alexander II in Russia.

148 — Pectoral shell necklace, Papua New Guinean, 20th century. Kina shell and plant fiber.

This carved shell necklace from Papua New Guinea likely arrived in Indonesia through trade. The island cultures, especially those far from the beaches in the Highland region, prized shells. Pectorals like these, worn as symbols of status, prosperity, and wealth, were traded as a form of currency.

149 (OPPOSITE) — Necklace, Eastern
Javanese, 12th century. Gold.

The curved shapes of this Javanese
necklace echo the designs of tiger claw
amulets worn in India, where stylized
claws are associated with the youthful
Hindu god Krishna and the Buddhist
bodhisattva Manjushri. A similar ornament,
dating from the early tenth century,
was found inside a jar in the vast
Wonoboyo hoard excavated in Central
Java in 1990.

150 — Hair pendants, Lhasa
Tibetan, 19th–early 20th century.
Silver and turquoise.

These stylish women's hair pendants—
made in the shape of lotus blossoms, or
akor—are examples of the Lhasa style,
once favored in the historic capital of
Tibet. Due to their considerable weight,
they would have been secured with hooks
to the hair or to a ceremonial headdress.
Similar pendants adorn the tombs of
Dalai Lamas in the Potala Palace, serving
as offerings.

151 — Simon Petiteau, armorial bracelet, about 1830. Gold, pearl, emerald, ruby, and diamond.

Written into this bracelet are layers of symbolism: a central baroque pearl forms a cavalryman's helmet with diamond and emerald plume, and patterns of emeralds and rubies set in yellow gold showcase military motifs. The piece was likely custom commissioned for the wife of a high-ranking officer in the French Foreign Legion, which, unlike the French Army, wears green.

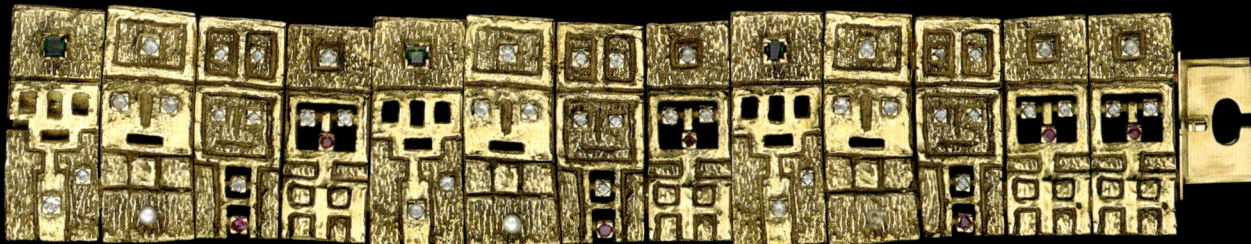

152 — Anton Frühauf, *King's Bracelet*, 1959. Gold, ruby, sapphire, tourmaline, and pearl.

Third-generation jeweler Anton Frühauf was one of the most influential goldsmiths in postwar Europe. This sculptural bracelet, its irregular surface illustrating a row of abstracted figures, showcases Frühauf's blend of traditional goldsmithing and Modernist aesthetics.

154 (OPPOSITE) — Pendant, Egyptian, 1070–712 BC. Gold and glass.

This pendant illustrates an ancient Egyptian creation myth: the sun god, Ra, emerging from a lotus blossom at dawn. Each element is laced with meaning. The tiny uraeus, or snake, on the child-king's forehead signifies his royal status and deepens the connection between the king and the young god.

153 — *Navaratna* (Nine gem) armlet, Indian, 19th century. Gold, enamel, ruby, emerald, sapphire, pearl, aquamarine, grossular garnet, amethyst, coral, citrine, turquoise, rose quartz, and metal-wrapped silk cord.

The nine-stone grid is a celestial symbol in Hindu cosmology that represents the universe's seven planets, as well as the ascending and descending nodes of the moon. Each of the stones is connected to an astral deity, or *navagraha*. The wearing of the nine stones together is thought to be auspicious and protective.

156 (OPPOSITE) — Necklace, North American or European, late 19th or 20th century. Jet and metal.

This highly polished necklace is a grand example of late nineteenth-century mourning jewelry. Victorian etiquette and rules of mourning dictated what to wear after the death of a loved one. Black "jet" jewelry, made of fossilized wood, was deemed appropriate throughout all stages of mourning, and became a popular accessory.

155 — Lisa Gralnick, *The Tragedy of Great Love*, 1994. Silver, gold, glass, salt, and sugar.

This locket opens to reveal a removable gold wedding band on one side and two granular substances on the other: sugar and salt. The two materials looked the same when the locket was first made, but eventually the salt will become corrosive, symbolizing the complex—and often contradictory—nature of love.

157 — Nancy Worden, *Runnin Yo Mama Ragged*, 1992. Silver, Plexiglas, and amethyst.

Seattle-based metalsmith Nancy Worden didn't shy away from feminist subjects; rather, she embraced them playfully. Titled *Runnin Yo Mama Ragged*, this brooch builds on the idea that "a mother's work is never done." It features six silver shoes spinning endlessly around a purple watch face.

158 — Jan Yager, *Dandelion*, 2001. Silver and auto glass.

In the 1990s, Jan Yager examined the urban landscape outside her North Philadelphia studio in the series *City Flora / City Flotsam*. Made from materials Yager found on the city sidewalk, *Dandelion* is a symbol of renewal that features broken auto glass, set like a gem, and large leaves patterned with tire treads.

159 — Asagi Maeda, *A Train Story*, 2008. Silver, gold, and resin.

Growing up in Tokyo, Asagi Maeda observed urban life through train windows. Here, she reverses that gaze, with scenes of daily life playing out inside a transparent vehicle. A poetic sort of timetable is engraved on the underside of the compartments, each train car a stanza: 6.00 (The first train), 8.00 (Rush hour), 10.00 (School trip), 12.00 (Gentle breeze), 14.00 (Sunshine), 16.00 (Kindness), 18.00 (Beautiful sunset), 20.00 (Emergency break), 22.00 (Night of a city), 24.00 (The last train), and 02.00 (The end of the day).

160 — Edward Everett Oakes, necklace, 1920s. Gold, pearl, and amethyst.

Early twentieth-century Boston makers like Edward Everett Oakes were known for their colorful hand-wrought jewelry. This necklace is reversible, with pearls on one side and amethysts on the other, and is closely related to Oakes's masterwork— a platinum and gem-set jewelry box Oakes completed and exhibited in October 1929.

161 — Edward Everett Oakes, jeweled casket, 1929. Silver, gold, amethyst, pearl, onyx, and laurel wood.

162 — Thierry Vendome, *Pluie* (Rain), about 2000. Iron, gold, and moonstone.

Thierry Vendome finds beauty in unexpected places. This pendant centers the rusted, twisted remains of an battered World War II tank found on the beaches of Normandy, France. Thinking about the D-Day invasions in 1944, Vendome topped the piece with cabochon moonstones in the form of water droplets.

EGYPTIAN PECTORAL

VICTORIA REED

Some writers have speculated that when Emma Hosford Stone sold an Egyptian pectoral, or breastplate, from her collection, to John Garrett in the nineteenth century, it was because she feared it was cursed (FIG. 163).[1] Her husband, George Alfred Stone, a civil and mechanical engineer from Boston, had bought it during a trip to Sheikh Abd el-Qurna in western Thebes (Egypt) in 1858, along with a scarab, a papyrus, and a tablet representing a "king upon his war-chariot."[2] He recounted in a letter of December 20, 1859:

> While at Thebes, I went out to shoot eagles, and one of the mountaineers who was with me said he could show me something better, and then produced the gold spread-eagle [pectoral], and wished me to buy it. I refused, thinking it was worth only its weight in gold. He came aboard my boat the next evening, and showed me the Papyrus and Tablet. I was then sure he had found the body of some person of consequence; so I purchased all three…. [Later] I sent my dragoman [translator and guide] back to Thebes to bring the man and anything of value he might have: and when he came, he produced the Scarabaeus, which I purchased.[3]

The seller told Stone that the objects had been found together, arranged on top of a mummy. This cannot be true, as scholars now believe the tablet and scarab are fake. A year earlier, archaeologist Alexander Henry Rhind had excavated a sealed tomb at Sheikh Abd el-Qurna, an event which probably facilitated the sale of artifacts with embellished stories to foreign buyers like Stone.

By 1873, the pectoral, along with the papyrus and tablet, found a home at Lafayette College in Easton, Pennsylvania. They were donated by alumnus John Garrett of Baltimore, Maryland, president of the B&O Railroad, who had purchased the pieces from Stone's wife. Why she sold the items to Garrett is unknown, but it was likely out of monetary need rather than superstition.

Bad luck nevertheless followed. In 1979, a college librarian stole the pectoral out of the Skillman Library at Lafayette.[4] He then entrusted it to a local dealer, who took it to the New York auction house Sotheby Parke-Bernet. At the time it was consigned for sale, in 1980, the pectoral had no documented provenance, or ownership history. There was only an anonymous, unsigned statement from the "owner" attesting that he had received it as a gift from his great-uncle before he died in 1945; since then, he claimed to have kept it either in his bedroom or in storage. In fact, he said it was only the recent interest in the King Tut exhibition—the blockbuster show that ran at The Metropolitan Museum of Art from 1978 to 1979—that reminded him he owned the pectoral in the first place, inspiring him to authenticate and sell it. His statement went on to include extraneous details a casual collector would have little reason to offer: for example, he noted that his great-uncle was a lifelong bachelor with an interest in the "unusual" who had amassed a "bizarre collection" during his travels.[5]

The story was, in many ways, too good to be true. If the pectoral really had been privately held since 1945,

then a buyer could be reassured that it was not recently looted from an archaeological site. It is also easy to believe that someone with no expertise in antiquities would have no formal documentation of the object's history. But there was no way to verify this convenient tale. The pectoral went unsold at auction, and the MFA bought it privately through Sotheby's a year later, in 1981, accepting the given provenance at face value—and without learning the identity of the consignor.

The MFA began conducting research on its new acquisition in the 1980s. At the same time, staff at Lafayette College realized the pectoral was missing, along with its accompanying documentation. Both institutions reached out separately to The Metropolitan Museum of Art, which happened to have a photograph of the pectoral on file, taken by a curator years earlier during

a routine visit to the college. By 1990, it was clear that the pectoral belonged to Lafayette, and the story offered by the anonymous consignor in 1980 was false.

In the early 1990s, cases of contested ownership were relatively rare—and certainly not expected. In what today seems a surprising move, the Museum asserted that it had good title to the pectoral, arguing that the statute of limitations on the crime had run out, and sued Lafayette to keep the piece. Lafayette countersued the MFA.

Few institutions want to find themselves in the middle of litigation. Given what we know today, we may ask: How could the Museum have avoided this situation? Since the late 1990s, the MFA has been conducting in-depth research into the history of its collection. The Museum has reached numerous voluntary ownership resolutions,

including returns, in response to claims of historical theft and looting. Through this process, art historians and researchers like myself have learned much more about the importance of due diligence, particularly when bringing a new object into the collection. We now know how crucial it is to verify accounts of ownership history before making a purchase. We know to look for suspicious "red flags," and, if something sounds too good to be true, we know that it probably is.

By 1992, both the MFA and Lafayette College had dropped their suits and agreed to a financial arrangement. Ownership of the pectoral was amicably transferred to the MFA, where it remains—not as a curse, but as a cautionary tale.

163 — Pectoral, Egyptian, 1783–1550 BC. Gold, silver, carnelian, and glass.

TV GUIDE

TANYA CRANE

Celebrated artist and jeweler Ron Ho is renowned for his distinctive approach to design that seamlessly blends cultural narratives with personal storytelling. Ho incorporates found objects in traditional jewelry-making techniques, a method which results in pieces that are not only visually striking but also rich in symbolism. One of his most notable creations, the *TV Guide* necklace, serves as a poignant example of his ability to reflect on contemporary culture through art (FIG. 164).

Ho's journey into the world of jewelry began with a deep appreciation for the stories objects tell. Born in Hawai'i and later based in Seattle, his multicultural background influenced his artistic perspective. The artist was particularly inspired by his travels in Asia, where he developed a keen interest in the cultural significance of everyday objects. His work often reflects a dialogue between Eastern and Western aesthetics, exploring themes of identity, cultural exchange, and the passage of time.

I was introduced to Ron Ho's work during a bead society meeting in Seattle in the early 2000s, a time when I was eager to immerse myself in the local art scene after moving there from Southern California. Seattle's jewelry scene was tight-knit, with artists frequently gathering to share their work and insights. This particular meeting was transformative for me, as Ho shared stories of his travels, his deep connections with other artists like Ramona Solberg and Laurie Hall, and his unique approach to integrating narrative into jewelry.

The *TV Guide* necklace in the MFA's collection exemplifies Ho's keen observational skills and his ability to capture the essence of cultural phenomena. It features a meticulously crafted Chinese altar table adorned with various offerings, including a patinated copper bowl with silver joss (incense) sticks, a television set, and vessels made of silver and Fimo clay. The jeweler found inspiration for the piece while visiting a commune in Taiwan, where he observed a striking scene: a family altar and a television set placed side by side. This juxtaposition highlighted the changing nature of reverence in contemporary life, where technology often assumes a central role. By placing the TV at the center of his own composition, Ho emphasized its prominence in the household, suggesting that it has become a modern-day object of worship, rivaling traditional spiritual practices.

As I delved deeper into Seattle's contemporary jewelry scene in the early 2000s, I frequently visited the Facèré Jewelry Art Gallery downtown. The gallery had become a cornerstone for the study of contemporary jewelry, showcasing a diverse array of materials, fabrication techniques, and the unique stories artists were telling through their work. It was here that I truly marveled at the depth and creativity within the local jewelry scene. Ho's influence on the community was palpable, not only in the aesthetic choices of many artists, but also in their approach to storytelling through jewelry.

It was clear, however, that while many artists were inspired by Ho, they were also forging their own paths, working in collaboration with both their own narratives and the broader culture of Seattle. This synergy created a vibrant tapestry of contemporary jewelry that was both individualistic and interconnected. Facèré Gallery was a testament to the strength of the city's jewelry community, a place where Ho's legacy lived on and evolved through the hands of other artists.

In reflecting on Ho's work, I see parallels with my own artistic journey. As a biracial African American woman, my work centers around my personal stories and experiences of navigating life between the predominantly white suburb of Los Angeles and South Central Los Angeles. Through my art, I narrate —literally—my fraternal ancestors' stories, using enamel and a sgraffito marking technique on symbolic objects. In doing so, I embed narratives into enamel jewelry, juxtaposed with found objects, to create pieces that are rich with historical and personal significance.

Two of my works, *Miguel's Story* and *Big Pimpin'*, are included in the collection of the MFA Boston (SEE FIG. 179). These pieces, like Ho's, explore themes of identity and heritage, though from a different cultural perspective. Just as Ho sought to connect with his Chinese heritage through his work, I strive to connect with the Black side of my family, using storytelling to bridge the gap between past and present, and to honor the complex, multifaceted history of my ancestors.

Ho's work challenges conventional notions of jewelry as mere adornment. Instead, he views the medium as a vehicle for storytelling and cultural critique. His pieces often engage with themes of consumerism, identity, and the shifting landscapes of tradition and modernity. *TV Guide*, for instance, is a wearable statement, prompting viewers to reflect on the pervasive influence of technology in our lives. The necklace, when worn on the body, becomes a conversation starter, accessible to a wide audience.

Ron Ho's *TV Guide* is a compelling exploration of cultural observations and the power of objects to convey meaning. Through his work, Ho invites us to reflect on our values, the objects we hold dear, and the evolving nature of worship and reverence in contemporary society. His ability to blend personal narrative with broader cultural commentary makes his work both unique and deeply resonant. The impact of his work extends beyond his own creations, influencing a generation of artists in Seattle and beyond, and continuing to inspire those who encounter his legacy.

164 (OPPOSITE) — Ron Ho, *TV Guide*, 1992. Silver, patinated copper, polymer clay, and silk cord.

LIBERTY

HELEN W. DRUTT ENGLISH

For over one half-century, Gijs Bakker has been involved in a diverse range of the arts beyond jewelry, including industrial design and urban planning. As critic Peter Dormer wrote in 1983, throughout Bakker's career, his craft aesthetic has integrated with his aesthetics of art and industrial design. In an interview for a 2005 monograph on his work with jewelry, Bakker expressed the importance of the art form in his life, saying, "I think, act and live through my jewelry."[1]

165 — Gijs Bakker, *Liberty,* 1997.
Silver and glass.

The idea of living through jewelry takes on particular meaning in Bakker's treatment of and transformations of portraiture, beginning in 1974 with a profile of his late wife, Emmy Van Leersum, and concluding in 2020 with a three-directional self-portrait. If one travels back in time, portraits appear often throughout Bakker's oeuvre—among them the *Curious* brooch, a 1999 frontal portrait of Benno Premsela, the "Kunst Pope of Amsterdam," his mirrored eyes expressing the designer and collector's flawless recognition of quality. In 1985, *The Tongue* appeared, a brooch unlike any other, which depicts a Black man with a protruding tongue balancing a diamond on its tip. In 2016's *Black to White*, Bakker used portraiture to challenge racial divides, creating a necklace which depicts fifteen of Bakker's male heroes arranged by skin tone and linked together, including Barack Obama and Leonardo DiCaprio, with Miles Davis next to David Bowie.

I had the opportunity to work with Gijs Bakker in 1997, when I commissioned the Dutch artist, celebrated for his unique position in modern and contemporary jewelry, to create a brooch for the exhibition *Brooching It Diplomatically*, a tribute to former Secretary of State Madeleine Albright's recognition of the power of brooches.[2] The work Bakker produced is yet another portrait, depicting the face of the Statue of Liberty with her crown, a reference to European royalty strengthened by its likeness to a halo and two clocks illustrating her eyes (FIG. 165).[3]

The exhibition was inspired by Alain L. Sanders's 1997 *Time* article "Brooching the Subject Diplomat-ically," which tells of an unusual strategy on the part of Albright, the first woman in American history to hold the position of Secretary of State. Albright announced her views with brooches, sending a variety of messages through her choices of jewelry. With her permission, I communicated with artists around the world—not to mention the Department of State—and expressed my desire to organize an invitational exhibition at my Philadelphia gallery in honor of Albright. Sixty-one artists from sixteen countries responded with seventy-one works remarkable for their creativity and inventiveness, as well as their humor, irony, and patriotism. Among them was Gijs Bakker's *Liberty*.[4]

The works of art in *Brooching It Diplomatically* were meant to be worn—not hidden in drawers or velvet boxes, but displayed as a symbol of position, a badge of honor, a mark of ritual experience, or for pure pageantry. They formed a visual connection between the artist, the wearer, and the audience. In a description of his brooch for the exhibition catalogue, Bakker wrote:

> *Liberty* is two real watches in an open structure. One watch is set upside down for Mrs. Albright to know how long her appointment will last and the other for her visitor to know when to leave. Of course people may philosophize about peace, time, distance, diplomacy etc., etc. but I think that politics are very one-dimensional.[5]

Gijs Bakker's *Liberty* brooch attained a place of honor on the cover of the catalogue, where it was superimposed over a Timothy Greenfield-Sanders portrait of Albright (SEE FIG. 128). How was the catalogue conceived? The designer Jari Silvennoinen worked in Helsinki under the auspices of Marianne Aav, the late Finnish director of the Designmuseo, who supported the exhibition and catalogue, also titled *Brooching It Diplomatically*. Bakker, who—quite by chance—was on a design pursuit, visited Jari on my behalf to sanction the book design— no wonder *Liberty* resides on the cover! His brooch also appeared on the cover of *Read My Pins*, an illustrated memoir and social history written by Albright in 2009. *Liberty* became an international symbol for the Secretary of State.

Gijs's work for *Brooching It Diplomatically* was not my first encounter with the artist. My first meeting with him took place in Philadelphia in 1973, the year before he created his first portrait of Emmy, and the year I opened my gallery. Gijs, Emmy, and their two-year-old son, Aldo, visited the city while on a lecture tour following Bakker's residency at Haystack Mountain School of Crafts in Maine. Honored was I by their visit; horrified were they by the American ceramics of Tom Rippon and the jewelry of Stanley Lechtzin, Olaf Skoogfors, and Albert Paley, so far removed from the spare Dutch aesthetic (SEE FIG. 60).

We bonded nevertheless. Our friendship is even stronger today, my archive of letters, photographs and faxes—now replaced with emails and phone calls—holding the history of a half-century-long personal and professional relationship. *Liberty* reigns high over it all, not simply as a brooch symbolizing freedom, but as an anchor which binds Gijs and me forever.

TASSEL EARRINGS

MELANIE GRANT

166 — Hemmerle, tassel earrings, 2018.
Iron, gold, and sapphire.

Once, deep in the darkness of a centuries-old cellar and hidden away by history in the German city of Munich, lay a couple of embossing stamps bearing the likeness of a crown. These stamps, or "molds," were surrounded by blocks of glossy wood, waiting for their turn to be transformed into resplendent body sculpture by jewelers Hemmerle—the owners of both the cellar and its contents. The molds may have given up hope of ever springing to life again, concealed by wood and obscurity, if not for Yasmin Hemmerle, who, after walking past them day after day, suddenly stopped to listen to their whispers.

The molds once produced crowns that sat atop medals honoring the brave—the workshop still makes the Bavarian Order of Merit today—but in Christian and Yasmin Hemmerle's hands, they were destined for more artful things (FIG. 167). Under the magical fingers of a single master goldsmith in their workshop, the embossing stamps were transformed into earrings, blending both Berlin iron jewelry from the studio's past with the jewels of distinction of their present (FIG. 166). Midnight blue sapphire beads strung onto hand-dyed silk threads were hung suspended from a dome, allowing each to sway seductively in the signature Hemmerle tassel style. Iron crowns slotted snugly over a curve of sapphires, combining matte blackness and twinkling blue light. The molds were alive once more.

"Iron provided that first spark into the freedom to use any material possible," says current and fourth-generation custodian Christian Hemmerle as he perches on a velvet

chair opposite his wife, Yasmin.[1] In 1995, when his parents, Stefan and Sylveli, took over the workshop, they shifted its focus to the art of jewelry, compelling an important collector "who detested flashy gems" to commission a diamond ring set in textured iron. This replacement alluded to the War of Liberation (1813–15), when patriotic Germans donated their gold to the war effort and wore neoclassical iron jewelry in its place. Christian and Yasmin then had their own epiphany in 2004 at an Yves Saint Laurent exhibition in Paris dedicated to the creative dialogue the designer had with the painters he loved. They

realized that every interpretation and inspiration yielded from art, nature, architecture, or design resulted in something new. In their eyes, observers of a work should be able to see the jewel's entire journey, from mold to work of art, in order to truly understand it.

The Hemmerles doubled down on art as inspiration, creating a style that is uniquely theirs, framed by the Bauhaus movement and Jugendstil naturalism, the German counterpart to Art Nouveau. "We've created a language, and we're continuously developing," says Yasmin. As part of their studio's current evolution, they moved to a new space in

Munich to allow their collectors more time and access to the craft. The engineering of their jewelry connects them, body and soul, to the final pieces, with every part of the design process openly discussed and considered. As the Hermmerles' expansion continues, twisting and turning with each new generation, the molds come into the light.

167 (ABOVE) — Nineteenth-century Hemmerle embossing stamps and samples alongside Grand Cross medal of the Order of Merit of the Bavarian Crown, 2018.

JEWELRY
IN THE MUSEUM

A CONVERSATION
WITH KENDALL REISS

Most art museums have jewelry in their collections. What makes the MFA unique, however, is that in addition to caring for a world-renowned jewelry collection, the Museum has a curator of jewelry—the only position of its kind in a North American fine art museum—as well as a dedicated jewelry gallery. Jewelry entered the MFA's collection in the institution's infancy, more than 150 years ago; more recently, the Museum has strategically added to its holdings, collecting design drawings, for example, and maintaining a library as a resource for scholars, artists, and educators.

Kendall Reiss, Professor of the Practice in Metals and Chair of 3D and Performance at the School of the Museum of Fine Arts at Tufts University (SMFA), and the author recently sat down to talk more about jewelry in the Museum: storytelling; the magic of close looking; and what jewelry can teach us about people, history, and culture.

KENDALL REISS The MFA's jewelry collection is so important and dynamic, especially when you think about how many conversations are within and among the objects themselves. I know you've expressed that an important part of your role as Rita J. Kaplan and Susan B. Kaplan Senior Curator of Jewelry is engaging with the community itself: focusing on the people that bring these objects into being—the makers—in addition to exploring how these objects hold history, knowledge, and lineages of material, of wearers, of the people who have loved these things.

I used to commute by train to Boston in my early days of teaching, around the time we first met. I would sit on the train and look at people's jewelry and think about the stories they told. In your role, it's really critical that you act as a communicator for these pieces and for the people that have made them. When you think about the MFA's collection, what are some of the stories that these objects can tell us?

EMILY STOEHRER I always think about who wore these things—where they wore them, what they wore them with. That might feel so obvious, because it's how we wear jewelry and how we live with jewelry. But in terms of the study of jewelry and the making of jewelry, the wearing isn't always the first thing that's considered. It often is those other themes, the themes of communication or of decorative arts, that come first.

For some people, it was kind of strange that I thought about adornment and fashion first. This idea clicked for me when, a few years ago, Sienna Patti, who has a gallery in Lenox, Massachusetts, approached me with the offer of a gift of seventy-nine charms from artists she'd worked with over her twenty-year career. We spoke about how important it felt that they be put on a bracelet

168 — Pendant with ram-headed sphinx on a column, Nubian, 743–712 BC. Gilded silver, lapis lazuli, and glass.

169 — Barbara Seidenath for Sienna Patti, *Sienna 201999*, 2019. Sterling silver and enamel.

for display. Charm bracelets carry memories, and while this one will never be worn, it felt important to put the charms on a bracelet to demonstrate each one's connection to the body. The work is titled *Charmed*, but I really think of it as "Sienna's Bracelet"—each small charm is a love letter from the artist to Sienna (FIGS. 169–70).

KR We've just seen another Met Gala, and people are thinking about the flamboyant and the contemporary—really the cutting edge—of adornment, this idea that jewelry has been around for so long. And this collection is representative of some of the earliest forms of jewelry that we can think of: the Egyptian broad collar and the Nike earring being two examples (SEE FIGS. 13, 9). And alongside that, considering developments in technology that allow for this work to emerge and reanimate in these different ways—the amazing craft that went into creating the tiny beads in the broad collar necklace or the beadnet dress, for instance (FIGS. 71, 167).

ES Technology is the reason that our ancient Egyptian and Nubian collections exist the way that they do. And I know that excavations are something that people struggle with hearing and talking about today, but we excavated this material in the Nile Valley starting in the nineteenth century. The person who was running those excavations was a man named George Reisner. He was the head of our Egyptian department at the time, and he utilized photography, which at the time was a new technology, to document the MFA's excavations.

170 — Sienna Patti, *Charmed*, 2019. Sterling silver.

171 — Beadnet dress, Egyptian, 2551–2528 BC. Faience.

172 — Harvard University—Boston Museum of Fine Arts Expedition, jewelry found at pyramids of Kashta, Piye, Shebitku, and Tanutamani, in El Kurru, Nubia (present-day Sudan), 1919.

This decision had a tremendous impact on the jewelry that they found, because much of it was made of beads, but all the stringing was gone. Through those photographs, curators have been able to put the jewelry back together, and that's allowed objects like the sphinx amulet, broad collar, and the lattice-work dress to be displayed as they were originally intended, rather than as groups of loose beads—and that is really exciting (FIGS. 172, 168).

KR This idea of bringing something back to life is really amazing. We've talked about this in our many conversations over the years—the ephemerality of some of these materials, and the knowledge that something made of fiber will break down eventually. That conservation piece is something that you have to think about a lot.

ES There are certain conservation requirements to consider. For *Beyond Brilliance*, I couldn't feature many examples with textiles, photos, and other materials that can't be exposed to light or on view for a very long time. Here in the book, I was able to include some of those objects that cannot be displayed long-term in the gallery.

There are some examples with textiles in the gallery because I had conversations with artists, most notably Elizabeth James Perry. We were talking about her *Medallion* necklace, which includes a naturally dyed leather element that would fade and show degradation over time (FIG. 174). She encouraged me to think about including it even though there were conservation risks. She explained that there would always be someone in her community, if not her, who could come back and fix it. Perry described that she would rather it be out and live and be seen, rather than stored away because of conservation needs.

That conversation opened up my mind. If I had cut out all the textiles in the gallery, her necklace would not have been on exhibit, among others: a beautiful Iranian amulet with writings from the Qur'an on the bottom, or an Indian *Navaratna* that was worn tied around the upper arm with gold and silk threads (FIG. 173).

So many times, just American and European stories get told in jewelry gallery spaces. These other objects are just as important to the story of jewelry, and their inclusion here allows for a broader history to be told. Working closely with conservators, we agreed that we would monitor them to make sure that they continued to be in good shape, and if they weren't, we would take them out. I felt it was important for them to be there. They look gorgeous alongside other examples of metalwork in the collection, and illustrate the many materials artists have used to make jewelry.

KR   This idea of the global context—can you speak more to that? There's a specificity within the objects themselves. Some of the ways that we think about global connection might come through materials or craft practices or oral traditions. What are your curatorial ideas around that?

ES   The MFA has a strong ancient jewelry collection, and then we don't have much until you get to the nineteenth century. There's a big gap. It made it impossible to organize things chronologically—in both the gallery and the book—but it opened up a much more interesting avenue to examine things thematically, and offered the chance to put unexpected objects together. Through that, you realize that there are these threads that run throughout history and throughout cultures around the globe.

We've had jewelry in our collection dating back to our founding years. The MFA was founded in 1870 and opened in 1876. In the years in between the founding and the opening, we collected many things, including jewelry. So we have jewelry that goes that far back, but we hadn't been actively collecting jewelry with precious gemstones. When Yvonne [Markowitz] was thinking about how she was going to get people in the Museum to really understand jewelry with diamonds and gems, she recognized that Marjorie Merriweather Post's emerald and diamond brooch was an object that could tell many stories

173 (LEFT) — Amulet box, Iranian, 19th century. Turquoise, glass, silver, and silk.

174 (ABOVE) — Elizabeth James-Perry, *Medallion*, 2022. Wampum and walnut-dyed deerskin.

(SEE FIG. 1). I wrote quite a bit on this brooch—made by Oscar Heyman Bros. for Marcus & Co.—for this book, and described the ways in which it stands as a highlight of both our Islamic and jewelry collections. We are continually learning more about where it came from and its many lives before arriving at the MFA.

KR   Amazing.

ES   My colleague Laura Weinstein, the MFA's curator of Indian art and South Asian art, reminded me that the brooch's emerald, which was detailed with an iris in India in the seventeenth century, was carved during the same moment in history the Taj Mahal was built—and that the Taj Mahal isn't the white building that we think it is, but that it was actually covered in flowers, and that the Mughals were fascinated by flowers. They lived surrounded by gardens, and were looking closely at the natural world and copying it (FIG. 175). And when you look at the flower on the brooch, you see evidence of their interest in naturalism. It likely was put into a turban ornament in those years. Then, later, it was carved on the back in a different style of flower—a daisy— that's flatter, more two-dimensional.

This single object touches on mining in the Americas, colonization, Indian art, Islamic art, global trade and transportation, and the many lives of jewelry

175 — Muhammad Shah in a garden, about 1730–40.

objects. In the early twentieth century, some Maharaja became more interested in contemporary jewelry by Cartier and others than traditional jewelry set with carved gems like this emerald, and as a result, many Indian jewels were broken apart. That's how the emerald came to be bought by a merchant in Bombay— now Mumbai—in the 1920s before finding its way to New York, where Marcus & Co. transformed it into the brooch we see today.

All jewelry functions as a storytelling device. The newest jewel in the book, and in the gallery, is a brooch by the Mumbai-based jeweler BHAGAT (SEE FIG. 71).

KR   And it is exquisite.

ES   It's this little window called the *Jali* that's taken from Indian and Islamic architecture. Viren Bhagat was looking at architecture, specifically in Mumbai, where he describes being inspired by moss growing up the buildings and sun shining through these spaces (SEE FIG. 72). This brooch is a little treasure in the shape of a window. It features round emerald beads that are meant to evoke moss, along with sliced, portrait-cut diamonds that are so clear that they look like panes of glass. This unusual approach to diamonds is so indicative of BHAGAT's work. When exhibited next to the Post brooch, I hope it makes people think about jewelry differently and see these big, global connections.

KR   And across cultures, jewelry, though worn on the body, has this innate ability to also bring the architectural to mind. That's really fascinating. I often think about buildings as gigantic pieces of jewelry. We're moving through them. Our bodies are interacting with them in ways that aren't that different from what it means to put on a piece of adornment.

ES   So often jewelry is given or received as a gift, too. It carries all these deep personal meanings to the owner, but many of those themes carry even to someone who's just seeing it and doesn't know the story behind it.

KR   You have this deep understanding of these objects. How do you translate them into a book like this? What happens to these objects when they enter the collection? How do their stories continue to develop as they become a part of the MFA—as they are placed in context? I mean, knowing also that some of these things still have lives of travel, they might exist within the MFA's collection, but they might be loaned out to another museum and get to travel across the globe again.

ES   So often people think of objects in museums as being unused and kept in dark cabinets, and that's not true. In this book, there are about 100 works of art, and in the gallery, there are 160 works of art, yet the collection has 25,000 objects.

176 — Cast iron brooch, German, before 1849. Iron.

Now, 18,000 of those are ancient beads; even still, it's a big collection, but it's an active collection. As you know, one of the ways that it comes alive is in our study room, where students, artists, and educators come to learn more about these objects. It's an opportunity to look closely at the work of a specific artist—or a technique, or a time period, or a culture—and to learn. Recently, you brought a student in to look at Berlin iron work (FIG. 176).

KR She's a blacksmith and was doing a lot of work, specifically jewelry work, with iron. The ability for her to visit and to do close looking and be in proximity with these pieces that she had only ever seen in books—to be able to be so close to an object like that—was a really powerful experience. That idea of accessibility and the collection existing for the people—museums and institutions have a responsibility to provide opportunities like that. Curators do as well, and I know you take it very seriously, and you do an amazing job of helping people to really understand that they have the ability and are welcome to be a part of that research.

I remember being in the study room with you at different times when there were folks looking really intricately at hallmarks on different objects to try to understand more about their history and the lineage of makers that would've touched them and been in contact with them.

ES   That learning is a work in progress. We have a great stomacher brooch with emeralds that at one point were thought to be glass because they are a very pale green (SEE FIG. 77). Through scientific testing, we were able to confirm that they are in fact emeralds, but there's still more to discover. For example, the brooch is marked more than ten times. You can clearly see the marks, but we have not yet figured out who made it. Someday we will. This is not a static collection. There is always more to learn.

What we've tried to put together at the MFA is a jewelry resource center, which you and your students have been so active in utilizing, and I hope other people will visit as well. So we're not only acquiring jewelry, but wherever possible, we're also trying to acquire related drawings to allow people to think more about the making process. For example, there's a compact by Jean Schlumberger that was fabricated by the goldsmith Louis Féron. When you see the mold and then look at the object, you realize the art and craft that goes into making these objects (FIGS. 177–78).

177 (BELOW) — Louis Féron Inc., *Dahlia* dye press, 1957–64. Brass and zinc.

178 (RIGHT) — Jean Schlumberger and Louis Féron Inc. for Tiffany & Co., *Dahlia Compact*, 1959. Gold and sapphire.

KR It's true. We're so lucky to be neighbors. That has meant that we have this ability to bring our students into dialogue with these objects, which really allows them to develop, not only as makers, but also as conceptual thinkers, as people who are concerned about topics of the day.

We have so much to gain from close looking. It is magical to come into the study space and have these small group, or one-on-one, interactions. You're the interlocutor, right? You're sort of the communicator, or the bridge, between us and history, and that history could be very current. But as you say, we add to the archival understanding of these objects over time. And I think for students in particular to be able to access this material in this way, and to know that they can ask to see these things, and the answer will mostly be "Yes," is empowering. I've watched students gain so much from their experiences with you in that space. I think you've inspired a whole generation of humans.

ES I certainly hold a lot of the stories, but this book, as a companion to the jewelry gallery and all its related resources, aims to offer broader access to the collection. As we were working on the gallery, I kept saying that every object has a story to tell. People kept asking, "Emily, how are you going to tell *every* story?" I took this on as a kind of challenge, and wrote a label for every single piece in the gallery. I did it partly to get these stories out, but also because I understand there are people who know and love the Museum's collection and who are lucky to visit all the time, but there are also many people—and students in particular—who can't get here.

The MFA's website offers photographs, object stories and descriptions, videos, and audio tours—through this technology, the collection becomes an active resource for artists, educators, enthusiasts, collectors, and curators near and far.

KR I was excited to see the emerald in the Post brooch on the website, with this close-up video panning across the surface of the stone, so you can see the iris and the carving. It showed such a detailed view that allowed me to see it in a really different way than I had before.

What has it meant to create some of those learning opportunities, like videos and labels? I mean, there's so much research and a labor of love that goes into going down that rabbit hole, and trying to uncover as much as you can, but knowing that there's always going to be more.

ES The learning is never truly done. The idea of doing a video came from something the artist Tanya Crane often says to me (SEE FIG. 179). When she was on the faculty at the SMFA, she brought her students to the gallery each semester. Without fail, she would describe how much she wanted to see the back of the objects on view. Her voice was in the back of my head, and I thought, "Let's figure out a way for Tanya and her students to see the reverse of a few objects."

I also wanted to offer a way to show special or hidden elements. My colleagues hoped I would choose one or two jewels to animate in this way, but six was as low as I could go. I picked things like the emerald to encourage people to look closely in the gallery. There's a brooch from about 1890 by a French jeweler named Auger, and there's this large, beautiful corsage ornament with blossoms that are set en-tremblant, so they tremble to catch the light (SEE FIG. 78). In the video, viewers get to experience the dazzling effect. Hemmerle's tassel earrings sway, dancing back and forth (SEE FIG. 166). Asagi Maeda's *A Train Story* necklace glides across the screen (FIG. 159). The videos make the jewels come alive.

KR There's something remarkable about scale, too, that happens in those videos. As we think about examples of jewelry that are commonly worn, they're not enormous statement pieces, but humble things that people wear on their own body every day. There is something transportive about the way that you created those videos and thought about these objects in that level of detail and intricacy—it does open up this entire world.

ES Jewelry is small. You have to get close to really appreciate all those details.

KR There are so many dialogues between these objects, too. Joyce J. Scott's piece and her bead work, for example, in conversation with an Egyptian broad collar. These connections between materiality, between craft, do speak across immense generational spaces of time.

180 — Detail of Asagi Maeda, *A Train Story*, 2008 (fig. 159). Silver, gold, and resin.

ES Joyce J. Scott's *Adam and Eve* necklace, which she made in the 1980s, is amazing, and I love thinking about it in conversation with that Egyptian broad collar, which was made about 4,000 years ago (SEE FIGS. 13–14). Years ago, around 2014, Joyce came to do a talk at the Museum, and afterward Yvonne Markowitz and I walked her around. The Nubian exhibition *Gold and the Gods* had just opened, which included many beads. Joyce has spent so much of her career thinking about beads and looking at beads, and we took her into the Egyptian storage area and looked closely at drawer after drawer of beads with her.

She said, "You know, I have this piece I did with Art Smith." Yvonne and I both stopped—"You have what?" She was really interested in the way the MFA could position her work alongside the ancient work by Egyptian and Nubian artists and Black artists. And I think we've just begun to scratch the surface and think about how we can strengthen those connections.

Joyce reminded me how important it is to remember the humble bead, because it's not always about preciousness and expensive materials. I have two little kids, and sometimes it's the things children make you out of pasta, or whatever, that are the most precious. And these beads aren't costly, but they make something extraordinary. And artists like Joyce recognize the power of jewelry. There's a reason she was named a MacArthur Genius, right?

KR She is a treasure. You are working with rock stars. Seriously, you think about some of these objects as historical examples of the craft. These are things that survived because they were incredibly important, valuable, and precious. You're also working among this community of contemporary jewelers, which is diverse. It spans a lot of different ways of making and thinking.

With many of these objects, however, you'll never know the maker. You might know something about their shop or through the hallmarks. There may be some way to learn or access what's there historically, but what does it mean to work with contemporary artists, trying to preserve their voices in this moment? Someone like Joyce who is so important to our field, or Tanya [Crane], who is absolutely doing incredible things. Ron Ho, who passed in 2017. What does it mean to steward these makers as storytellers?

ES It's interesting. I have my hands in a lot of different fields, because jewelry is not one big tent. There are fine jewelers, costume jewelers, and contemporary jewelers, and they're not always talking to each other. One of the delights of my job is that I get to talk to everybody, and I get to think about all of this work coming together and speaking to each other. It's exciting to think about the stories these objects tell as a reflection of the current moment. The collection isn't stagnant, and these stories will evolve over time with each generation.

KR   That idea of longevity is something that is sitting with me. Jewelry—it is enduring. Some materials will exist many human lifetimes over, but this idea about extending the longevity of an object through storytelling or through the work of the Museum, to be able to document and share that, is so important. It's about accessibility, it's about people being able to truly engage with these objects on a much more personal level—they may resonate with something in a really different way than if they were looking solely at an image of it, or even if it were presented in person.

There's a lot more to knowledge than knowing. There is the getting to know, the being with. You have this opportunity to study things in a different way. It allows for a different level of engagement when you present these objects to people.

ES   What does it mean to you to have this access to the collection over the years? Has there been one, or maybe more than one, memorable moment?

KR   It's a dream, really. When I think about why museums or collections have been so important to my own practice, having that access in graduate school, being able to think about the history of adornment with the actual objects that were part of that history, resonates strongly with me. I have a geology background, and so I have always been a hands-on learner.

Going to graduate school and interacting with these objects was a gift— something that I, again, didn't know that I could do until someone gave me that permission. That was Barbara Seidenath, who was my instructor at RISD, and it's through Barbara that I found my way to the School of the Museum of Fine Arts in Boston (SEE FIG. 169).

When I began teaching, I felt really strongly about bringing students in to be able to give them that exact experience, to be able to help them understand their own access and that they can understand objects in this different way— the power of what that can provide a maker to understand better how something is put together.

We are often looking back to historical objects to understand mechanisms or different techniques, some of which have been lost to time, like granulation. They are able to be re-understood through a different context, brought back to life. I think there's something in it for me, that it's sort of paying it forward. This was a part of my own learning process that was important. Being able to pass that to my students has been magical.

ES   What other ways could you use the collection that you haven't explored yet with your students or in your own art practice?

171 — Paul Revere, Jr., wedding ring, 1773. Gold.

KR There's something so beautiful about both the idea of jewelry as something very mundane and sort of common—like a gold wedding band, something that is now ubiquitous in a lot of different capacities—but also, the specialization of what a collection like that can provide that we would never have access to see without a museum like the MFA (FIG. 171).

It's really a dream to be situated so closely. We're literally right across the street—we just pop over for lunch if we want to. More important, though, is the generosity of spirit that you have in understanding your responsibility to share your knowledge. It's a very generous act, and it's an act of caring for these objects and also the capacity of access and really bringing people into the collection as well as bringing the collection outward, whether that's learning more about the artist, or learning more about a process or a material or a historical context. I've watched a lot of students develop their own voices as makers through interacting with the MFA jewelry collection.

LIKE SO MANY OTHER MUSEUM COLLECTIONS, only a small fraction of the MFA's jewelry is on view in the public galleries. But, behind closed doors in book-lined offices, the entire collection remains vibrant. The stories told on these pages are the result of ongoing research by the author, museum professionals, and scholars in the field who are continually making new discoveries and considering objects from fresh perspectives.

The jewelry collection is continually examined, studied, and cared for. Far from static, the object details found on the MFA's website are constantly updated as new information becomes available. Each year, jewelry from the Museum travels to be featured in exhibitions around the globe, and is published in books and articles spanning a wide range of topics. It is brought out for close looking by visitors ranging from curators to students to makers. Just as Kendall Reiss's students were able to interact with these objects, with advanced planning, the MFA's jewelry collection and extensive art library is available to anyone. Appointments can be made to view items in the David and Roberta Logie Department of Fashion, Textiles, and Jewelry collection up close. What stories will these jewels reveal to you?

NOTES

COLLECTING JEWELRY AT THE MUSEUM OF FINE ARTS, BOSTON

1. Oppi Untracht, *Traditional Jewelry of India* (New York: Harry N. Abrams, 1997), 328, 760. More recent research by Kris Lane examines the emerald and trade between the Americas, Europe, and India in *Colour of Paradise: The Emerald in the Age of Gunpowder Empires* (New Haven: Yale University Press, 2010).
2. "Entertains with 'India Arts' Tea," *Montclair Times*, October 23, 1929, 16.
3. Between 2010 and 2020, the Rita J. and Stanley H. Kaplan Family Foundation Gallery featured five special exhibitions: *Gems, Jewels, and Treasures* (2011–14), *Gold and the Gods: Jewels of Ancient Nubia* (2014–17), *Past Is Present: Revival Jewelry* (2017–18), and *Boston Made: Arts and Crafts Jewelry and Metalwork* (2018–20). In the wake of 2020's pandemic, the gallery featured two singular installations: *From Paris to Hollywood: Claudette Colbert's Starfish Brooch* (2021–23) and *The Marlborough Gem* (2023–24).

MANY WAYS OF LOOKING

1. Marjan Unger, *Jewellery in Context: A Multidisciplinary Framework for the Study of Jewellery*, trans. Ton Brouwers (Stuttgart: Arnoldsche Art Publishers, 2019), 18.
2. Bruce Metcalf, "On the Nature of Jewelry," *Metalsmith*, Winter 1993, 22–27, 22.
3. Unger, *Jewellery in Context*, 19.
4. Unger, 82–83.
5. Charles Russell, *Art as Adornment: The Life and Works of Arthur George Smith* (Parker, CO: Outskirts Press, 2015), 161.
6. Lowery Stokes Sims, Dennis Carr, Janet L. Comey, et al., *Common Wealth: Art by African Americans in the Museum of Fine Arts, Boston* (Boston: MFA Publications, 2014), 170–71.

THE JEWELER'S ART

1. Cathleen McCarthy, "Joan Sonnabend's Artist-Made Jewelry on the Block," *Jewelry Loupe*, September 2012.
2. Susan Weber Soros et al., *Castellani and Italian Archeological Jewelry* (New Haven: Yale University Press, 2004), 10.
3. Charlotte Gere and Judy Rudoe, *Jewellery in the Age of Queen Victoria: A Mirror to the World* (London: British Museum, 2010), 400.
4. Gere and Rudoe, *Jewellery in the Age of Queen Victoria*, 401.
5. Geoffrey Munn, "Giacinto Melillo: A Pupil of Castellani," *Connoisseur*, September 1977, 20.
6. Soros et al., *Castellani and Italian Archeological Jewelry*, 417.

7. *The Golden Fleece Headpiece* was first exhibited in *What Is Luxury?* at London's Victoria and Albert Museum, April 25–September 27, 2015, and later featured in *Solid Gold* at the Brooklyn Museum in New York, from November 16, 2024–July 6, 2025.
8. For more on Farnham, see John Loring, *Paulding Farnham: Tiffany's Lost Genius* (New York: Harry N. Abrams, 2000).
9. Moore's collection and influences were examined in The Metropolitan Museum of Art's 2024 exhibition *Collecting Inspiration: Edward C. Moore at Tiffany & Co.* and the corresponding catalogue.
10. Ralph Bergengren, "Some Jewels and a Landscape," *House Beautiful*, April 1915, 149.
11. "Jewelry for People Who are Slightly Mad," pamphlet, Sam Kramer maker file, Museum of Fine Arts, Boston.
12. Mark Foley, "Fantastic Jewelry for People Who are Slightly Mad," *Metalsmith* 6, no. 1 (Winter 1886): 11.
13. Kelly H. L'Ecuyer and Michelle Tolini Finamore, "New Directions: International Jewelry, 1970–2000," *Jewelry by Artists: In the Studio, 1940–2000* (Boston: MFA Publications, 2010), 176–77.
14. Meeling Wong, Managing Director of Georg Jensen, as quoted by Zaha Hadid Architects, "Lamellae Collection for Georg Jensen," media release, July 27, 2016.
15. John Paul Cooper, "Design," quoted in N. Natasha Kuzmanović, *John Paul Cooper: Designer and Craftsman of the Arts and Crafts Movement* (Stroud, UK: Sutton Publishing, 1999), 101.
16. Betty Cooke quoted in Jeannine Falino, *The Circle and the Line: The Jewelry of Betty Cooke* (Lewes, UK: GILES and the Walters Art Museum, 2000), 19.

CHICLET NECKLACE AND MOSAIC CUFF

1. I am grateful to Angie Reano Owen for the conversations that led to this essay, especially the recorded interview with the author and Ken Williams Jr. on July 17, 2024.

FOREVER DANCING—BRIGHT STAR

1. All quotes in this essay are from an email interview the author conducted with Wallace Chan in July 2024.

JALI

1. Qur'an 24:35.

BODY AS CANVAS

1. Art Smith quoted by Lee Nordness, *Objects USA: Works by Artist-Craftsmen in Ceramic, Enamel, Glass, Metal, Plastic, Mosaic, Wood and Fiber* (New York: Viking Press, 1970), 208.

2. Marjan Unger, *Jewellery in Context: A Multidisciplinary Framework for the Study of Jewellery*, trans. Ton Brouwers (Stuttgart: Arnoldsche Art Publishers, 2019).
3. Colbert won the Academy Award for Best Actress on February 27, 1935. In 1938, the income tax poll named her the highest-paid woman in America with a salary of $426,944. "My Income: One Minute with Claudette Colbert," *Photoplay*, October 1940, 73.
4. In 1938, from January until May, Claudette Colbert and Jack Pressman took a second honeymoon. Traveling through Austria, England, Egypt, France, Italy, and Switzerland, they spent two weeks in Paris. The media covered her trip closely. Despite telling the media that "shopping was taboo," almost immediately upon arriving in Paris, Colbert was seen shopping on Avenue de la Opéra, the same street where Boivin was located. "Claudette Colbert Selects Flowered Voile Underwear," *Corpus Christi Caller-Times*, May 11, 1938, 14.
5. Mayme Peak, "Hollywood's $1,000,000 Girl: Claudette Colbert, Highest Paid Star, Receives More Money Than Her Bosses, But She Can Save Only a Little of It," *Daily Boston Globe*, July 21, 1940, C5.
6. Françoise Cailles, *René Boivin: Jeweller*, trans. Tanya Leslie (London: Quartet Books, 1994), 269.
7. Cailles, *René Boivin*, 6.
8. "She Couldn't Afford a Date: But those days are over, for now Claudette Colbert gets what she wants when she wants it," *Modern Screen*, August 1939, 86.
9. Gwenn Walters, "Photoplay Fashions: Luxurious Furs," *Photoplay*, November 1939, 53.
10. Edmonde Charles-Roux, *Chanel and Her World: Friends, Fashion, Fame* (New York: Vendome Press, 2005), 377.
11. Translations and research conducted by Tzu-Ju Chen, Curatorial Research Associate for Jewelry, was essential in the understanding and interpretation of this object. It's possible the belt had more plaques at one time, but with seven jade elements, this is a spectacular and rare example of this form from this early period.
12. Queen Mary, note accompanying Japanesque brooch (2009.2533), 1952. Ink on paper, embossed. Museum of Fine Arts, Boston.
13. For more on this early history, see Deanna Farnetti Cera, *Adorning Fashion: The History of Costume Jewellery to Modern Times* (Melton, UK: ACC Art Books, 2019).
14. Deanna Farnetti Cera, "The Luxury of Freedom, the Freedom of Luxury: The United States, 1935–1968," *Jewels of Fantasy: Costume Jewelry of the 20th Century* (New York: Harry N. Abrams, 1991), 149–200.

15. Many examples of costume jewelry are marked with US patent numbers or patent pending numbers. These numbers correspond to design drawings or mechanisms, like clasps, closures, or the frames used to hold double-clip brooches. For example, the frame that holds Coro's *Duette* by Adolph Katz together as a single pin is marked PAT. No. 1798867. A digital search at the United States Patent and Trademark Office identifies this number as corresponding to a design for the frame and pinstem by Gaston Candas of Paris, France, for this "Brooch and the Like," filed on May 31, 1930.

16. Patricia Corbett, *Verdura: The Life and Times of a Master Jeweler* (New York: Thames & Hudson, 2002), 52.

17. "All that Glitters," *Vogue*, February 1933, 42–43 and Patrick Mauriès, *Jewelry by Chanel* (New York: Bulfinch Press, 1999), 19–20.

18. The necklace was photographed on a model in "Chanel Today," *Women's Wear Daily*, January 25, 1983, 4.

19. Dean Merceron, *Lanvin* (New York: Rizzoli, 2007), 310.

20. Charles Russell, *Art as Adornment: The Life and Works of Arthur George Smith* (Parker, CO: Outskirts Press, 2015), 161.

21. *From the Village to Vogue*, curated by Barry R. Harwood, Curator of Decorative Arts, Brooklyn Museum, May 14, 2008–June 19, 2011; Lynn Yeager, "Modern Master: Silver Streak," *Vogue*, December 2007, 218.

22. June Weir, "Women of Fashion," *New York Times Magazine*, April 11, 1982, 45.

23. Clare Phillips, *Bejeweled by Tiffany, 1837–1987* (Chicago: Art Institute of Chicago, 2006), 292.

GOLDFINGER

1. Helen W. Drutt English, conversation with the author, July 29, 2024.

2. Carla Gallo Barbisio, "The Observation of Artists," in *Martinazzi* (Turin: Stamperia Artistica Nazionale, 1990), 43.

3. Barbisio, "Chronology," in *Martinazzi*, 67.

4. Drutt English, conversation with the author, July 29, 2024.

5. Barbisio, "Chronology," 67.

6. Barbisio, "Chronology," 67.

STATEMENT JEWELS

1. Madeleine Albright to Eleanor Clift, "Madeleine Albright on the Pins She Wore," *Newsweek*, September 27, 2009.

2. Yvonne J. Markowitz, *Artful Adornment: Jewelry from the Museum of Fine Arts, Boston* (Boston: MFA Publications, 2011), 89.

3. Made to resemble a cameo, which are usually carved from hardstone or shell, Wedgwood's black and white design was made of ceramic.

4. Josiah Wedgwood to Benjamin Franklin, February 29, 1788, in *The Papers of Benjamin Franklin*, Packard Humanities Institute, American Philosophical Society, and Yale University, franklinpapers.org.

5. Carla Ginelli Brunialti and Robert Brunialti, "Patriotic Jewelry," in *American Costume Jewelry: Art & Industry, 1935–1950*, vol. 2 (Atglen, PA: Schiffer Publishing, 2008), 237.

6. Brunialti and Brunitalti, "Patriotic Jewelry," 232.

7. Dr. Christa Clarke wrote about this broad collar, and the powerful statement Mandela made in choosing to wear a similar necklace, in "Beaded collar (*ingqosha*), Xhosa artist, South Africa," in *Art of Africa*, Smarthistory, January 31, 2023.

8. Clarke, "Beaded collar (*ingqosha*)."

9. Eleanor Clift, "Madeleine Albright on the Pins She Wore," *Newsweek*, September 27, 2009.

10. Peter Lacovara and Yvonne J. Markowitz, *Nubian Gold: Ancient Jewelry from Sudan and Egypt* (Cairo: American University of Cairo Press, 2019), 122.

11. Yvonne J. Markowitz, *Artful Adornment: Jewelry from the Museum of Fine Arts, Boston* (Boston: MFA Publications, 2011), 32.

12. Thank you to Simona Di Nepi, Charles and Lynn Schusterman Curator of Judaica at the MFA, Boston, for helping me to understand the historical and religious significance of this ring.

13. Mark E. Neeley, Jr., and R. Gerald McMurty, *The Insanity File: The Case of Mary Todd Lincoln* (Carbondale, IL: Southern Illinois University Press, 1986), 15, describes that toward the end of 1864 Lincoln purchased $3,200 worth of jewelry at Galt's.

14. Neeley and McMurty, *The Insanity File*, 127–35.

15. "Disgraceful," *Clarksburg Conservative*, November 9, 1867, 6.

16. Documentation shared with the bracelet's owner when it was purchased, titled "*Enuh: Life Bracelet* by Lyndon Tsosie (Navajo) as told to Susan Pourian by Lyndon Tsosie," on letterhead from the Indian Craft Shop, US Department of the Interior, Washington, DC.

17. Lyndon Tsosie, phone call with the author, December 1, 2023.

18. Tsosie, phone call with the author, 2023.

19. "*Enuh: Life Bracelet* by Lyndon Tsosie (Navajo) as told to Susan Pourian by Lyndon Tsosie," US Department of the Interior, Washington, DC.

20. Henrietta Lidchi, *Surviving Desires: Making and Selling Native American Jewelry in the American Southwest* (Norman: University of Oklahoma Press, 2015), 139.

21. Charlotte Gere and Judy Rudoe, *Jewellery in the Age of Queen Victoria: A Mirror to the World* (London: British Museum, 2010), 27–29.

22. The eagle is referred to as the Coburg eagle in the *Journal of Mary Frampton*, ed. H. G. Mundy (London: Sampson Low, Marston, Searle & Rivington, 1885), 412. This name was later repeated in Shirly Bury's book *Jewellery: The International Era, 1789–1910*, vol. 1 (Melton, UK: Antique Collector's Club, 1991), 309. However, British Museum curators question if there is any connection to the Coburg coat of arms or if it was instead meant to be the German Imperial eagle. See British Museum 2002,0301.1, "brooch," 1839–40, britishmuseum.org.

23. Anna Tabakhova, *4,000 Years of Fasteners in Jewellery* (Paris: Éditions Terracol, 2017), 230–31.

24. *Madame de Pompadour: Patron and Printmaker*, Walters Museum of Art, Baltimore, MD, February 28, 2016–May 29, 2016. *A Suite of Prints Engraved by Madame the Marquise de Pompadour after the Carved Gems of Jacques Guay* is part of the collection of the Walters Museum in Baltimore, and was exhibited in 2016. Numbering around twenty prints, made about 1755, this is the only complete set that is known.

25. Tabakhova, *4,000 Years of Fasteners in Jewellery*, 230–31.

EGYPTIAN PECTORAL

1. See, for example, Peter Lacovara, "An Ancient Egyptian Royal Pectoral," *Journal of the Museum of Fine Arts, Boston* 2 (1990): 22; Art Jahnke, "The Curse of the Gold Vulture," *Boston Magazine*, August 1991, 81.

2. G[ustavus] Seyffarth, "A Remarkable Papyrus Scroll," *Transactions of the Academy of Science of St. Louis* 1 (1856–60): 528.

3. George A. Stone to G[ustavus] Seyffarth, December 20, 1859, in *Transactions of the Academy of Science of St. Louis* 1 (1856–60): 689.

4. For a full discussion, see Jahnke, "The Curse of the Gold Vulture," 78–81, 117–18, 120–21.

5. Museum of Fine Arts, Boston, Art of Ancient Egypt, Nubia, and the Near East, curatorial file, 1981.159, 1981.

LIBERTY

1. Yvonne Joris and Ida Van Zijl, *Gijs Bakker and Jewelry* (Stuttgart: Arnoldsche Art Publishers, 2007), 45–46.

2. The *Liberty* brooch is an edition of five. The MFA's brooch is the first in the series.

3. Gijs Bakker, email message to author, July 24, 2024.

4. Text adapted from my essay in the exhibition catalogue. See Helen W. Drutt English, "Introduction," *Brooching It Diplomatically: A Tribute to Madeleine K. Albright* (Stuttgart: Arnoldsche Art Publishers, 1998), 4–5.

5. Bakker quoted in Drutt English, "Introduction," 26.

TASSEL EARRINGS

1. Christian and Yasmin Hemmerle, interview with the author, June 27, 2024.

LIST OF ILLUSTRATIONS

Unless otherwise noted, objects are in the collection of the Museum of Fine Arts, Boston. Dimensions given are each object's largest measurement, whether height, width, length, or diameter.

COLLECTING JEWELRY AT THE MUSEUM OF FINE ARTS, BOSTON

1
Emerald and diamond brooch (known as the Post Brooch), 1929
Oscar Heyman Bros. (American, founded 1912)
For Marcus & Co. (American, 1892–1941)
Platinum, diamond, and emerald
5.4 cm (2 ⅛ in.)
William Francis Warden Fund, Marshall H. Gould Fund, Frank B. Bemis Fund, Mary S. and Edward J. Holmes Fund, John H. and Ernestine A. Payne Fund, Otis Norcross Fund, Helen and Alice Colburn Fund, William E. Nickerson Fund, Arthur Tracy Cabot Fund, Edwin E. Jack Fund, Frederick Brown Fund, Elizabeth Marie Paramino Fund in memory of John F. Paramino, Boston Sculptor, Morris and Louise Rosenthal Fund, Harriet Otis Cruft Fund, H. E. Bolles Fund, Seth K. Sweetser Fund, Helen B. Sweeney Fund, Ernest Kahn Fund, Arthur Mason Knapp Fund, John Wheelock Elliot and John Morse Elliot Fund, Susan Cornelia Warren Fund, Mary L. Smith Fund, Samuel Putnam Avery Fund, Alice M. Bartlett Fund, Benjamin Pierce Cheney Donation, Frank M. and Mary T. B. Ferrin Fund, and Joyce Arnold Rusoff Fund, 2008.179
Reproduced with permission

2
Portrait of Marjorie Merriweather Post, 1944
Yousuf Karsh (Armenian Canadian, 1908–2002)
Gelatin silver print
24.5 cm (9 ⅝ in.)
Hillwood Estate, Museum & Gardens, Archives and Special Collections, Bequest of Marjorie Merriweather Post, 1973
© Estate of Yousuf Karsh

3
Bishop's ring, 18th century
Probably English
Gold, sapphire, and diamond
2.2 cm (⅞ in.)
William D. Boardman Collection—Gift of Mrs. Alice L. Boardman, 01.5943

4
Beads, about 1700–1550 BC
Nubian, Classic Kerma, found in Sudan, Kerma, Cemetery S, K, IV, K 420, body C
Faience
0.3 cm (⅛ in.) each
Harvard University—Boston Museum of Fine Arts Expedition, 13-12-302

5
Link bracelet, about 1948
Winifred Mason Chenet (American, 1913–1993)
Copper and brass
15.2 cm (6 in.)
Museum purchase with funds donated by Stephen Borkowski, 2021.1057

6
Design for a necklace, about 1920
Frank Gardner Hale (American, 1876–1945)
Graphite on paper
21.6 cm (8 ½ in.)
Museum purchase with funds donated by Jean S. and Frederic A. Sharf, an anonymous donor, and the George Peabody Gardner Fund, SC.Hale.4

7
Jeweled scroll brooch, about 1920
Frank Gardner Hale (American, 1876–1945)
Gold, zircon, diamond, sapphire, and peridot
6.6 cm (2 ⅝ in.)
Gift of Joseph B. and Edith Alpers, 1998.569

8
Cameo with the wedding of Cupid and Psyche or an initiation rite (known as the Marlborough Gem), 50–25 BC
Tryphon (Roman, life dates unknown)
Roman, Late Republican or Early Imperial Period
Onyx
4.5 cm (1 ¾ in.)
Henry Lillie Pierce Fund, 99.101

MANY WAYS OF LOOKING

9
Earring with Nike driving a two-horse chariot, about 350–325 BC
Northern Greek, Late Classical or Early Hellenistic Period
Gold and enamel
5 cm (2 in.)
Henry Lillie Pierce Fund, 98.788

10
Mary Lee Hu (American, born 1943)
Choker #88, 2005
Gold
21.6 cm (8 ½ in.)
The Daphne Farago Collection, 2017.4933
Reproduced with permission

11
Wood sautoir, 1940–49
Miriam Haskell Company (American, founded 1926)
Brass, wood, glass, and silk
78 cm (30 ¾ in.)
Gift of Carole Tanenbaum, 2018.4149

12
Ellington, about 1958
Art Smith (American, born in Cuba, 1917–1982)
Silver, turquoise, rhodonite, chalcedony, and amazonite
43.8 cm (17 ¼ in.)
The Daphne Farago Collection, 2006.537
Reproduced with permission

13
Wesekh broad collar, 2246–2152 BC
Egyptian, Old Kingdom, Dynasty 6, reign of Neferkara Pepy II, found in Tomb of Impy, G 2381 A
Gold, steatite, turquoise, and lapis lazuli
17.5 cm (6 ⅞ in.)
Harvard University—Boston Museum of Fine Arts Expedition, 13.3086

14–15
Adam and Eve, 1985
Joyce J. Scott (American, born 1948)
Glass, wire, and nylon
31.8 cm (12 ½ in.)
The Daphne Farago Collection, 2013.1721
Reproduced with permission

THE JEWELER'S ART

16
Disc-shaped earrings, 6th century BC
Etruscan
Gold
5 cm (2 in.) each
Musée du Louvre, Paris, France, BJ43;BJ44
© RMN-Grand Palais / Art Resource, NY

17
Brooch, about 1859
Castellani (Italian, 1814–1930)
Gold
5 cm (2 in.)
Bequest of Mrs. Arthur Croft—The Gardner Brewer Collection, 01.6505

18
Lion brooch, about 1870
Micromosaic probably by
Luigi Podi (died 1888)
For Castellani
(Italian, 1814–1930)
Gold and glass
10.2 cm (4 in.)
Gift of Susan B. Kaplan,
2021.756

19
Polyp Colony, 1995
John Paul Miller
(American, 1918–2013)
Gold and enamel
5.7 cm (2 ¼ in.)
The Daphne Farago Collection,
2006.361
Reproduced with permission

20
Spille, 1999
Giovanni Corvaja
(Italian, born 1971)
Platinum and gold
5 cm (2 in.)
Gift of Yoshiko Yamamoto in
honor of Yvonne J. Markowitz,
2014.2061

21–22
Thunderbird, 2009
Charlene Sanchez Reano
(San Felipe Pueblo, born 1960)
Frank Reano (Kewa-San
Domingo Pueblo, 1962–2021)
Turquoise, spiny oyster shell,
jet, mother-of-pearl, lapis
lazuli, and melon shell
40.6 cm (16 in.)
Gift of V. Howard, 2021.326

23
Jaguar effigy pendant,
700–1520
Diquís (Costa Rica)
Gold-copper alloy,
5.7 cm (2 ¼ in.)
Gift of the Leslie S. Feron
Trust, 2017.4268

24
Jaguar brooch, 1940–46
William Spratling
(American, 1900–1967)
Silver and amethyst
11.7 cm (4 ⅝ in.)
Gift of Jim and Penny Morrill,
2016.182

25
Apparitions, about 1899
Eugène Samuel Grasset
(French, born in Switzerland,
1841–1917)
For Henri Vever
(French, 1854–1942)
Gold and enamel
5 cm (2 in.)
William Francis Warden Fund,
2015.2162

26
Peace, 2011
Shinji Nakaba (Japan, born 1950)
Helmet shell, gold, and
stainless steel
8.3 cm (3 ¼ in.)
Museum purchase with funds
donated by Yvonne J. Markowitz
in honor of Toni Strassler, 2015.157
© Shinji Nakaba

27
Necklace, about 1910
Louis Comfort Tiffany
(American, 1848–1933)
For Tiffany & Co.
(American, founded 1837)
Opal, demantoid garnet,
sapphire, and gold
With chain: 59.7 cm (23 ½ in.)
William Francis Warden Fund,
2017.1328

28
Hand ornament, about 1893
G. Paulding Farnham
(American, 1859–1927)
For Tiffany & Co.
(American, founded 1837)
Gold, turquoise, sapphire, garnet,
zircon, peridot, beryl, tourmaline,
chrysoberyl, and pearl
33 cm (13 in.)
Gift of Jody Sataloff in memory
of Joseph and Ruth Sataloff,
2019.2199

29
Necklace, 1910–18
Josephine Hartwell Shaw
(American, 1865–1941)
Gold, jade, and glass
10.2 cm (4 in.)
Gift of Mrs. Atherton Loring,
1984.947

30
Bangles, late 1930s
Marie Zimmermann
(American, 1878–1972)
Gold, jade, carnelian, and
enamel
6.2 cm (2 ½ in.) each
Museum purchase with funds
donated by the Rita J.
and Stanley H. Kaplan Family
Foundation, 2014.395.1-2
© MZ Archive

31
Madame Jean Lassalle wearing
jewelry by Jean Fouquet and a
hat by Madame Agnès
Published in *L'Officiel de la
couture, de la mode de Paris*,
1929
D'Ora (Dora Kallmus,
Austrian, 1881–1963)
Gelatin silver print
Paris, Musée des Arts
Décoratifs
© MAD, Paris

32
Art Deco brooch, about 1925–30
United States, based on a
1925 design by Jean Fouquet
(French, 1899–1984)
Silver, lapis lazuli, and onyx
6.7 cm (2 ⅝ in.)
Gift of Carole Tanenbaum,
2018.4062

33
Machine Age necklace, 1930–37
Auguste Bonaz
(French, 1877–1922)
Chrome and plastic (Galalith)
8.5 cm (3 ⅜ in.)
Gift of Carole Tanenbaum,
2018.4066
Courtesy Primavera Gallery, NY

34
Girl Before a Mirror, 1989
Wendy Ramshaw
(British, 1939–2018)
Rings: silver and resin;
stand: nickel alloy and resin
17.1 cm (6 ¾ in.)
The Daphne Farago Collection,
2006.462.1-10

35
Girl Before a Mirror, 1932
Pablo Picasso
(Spanish, 1881–1973)
Oil on canvas
162.3 cm (64 in.)
Museum of Modern Art, Gift
of Mrs. Simon Guggenheim,
2.1938
© 2025 Estate of Pablo Picasso / Artists
Rights Society (ARS), New York Digital
Image © The Museum of Modern Art /
Licensed by SCALA / Art Resource, NY

36
Lovers, 1949
Carol Kramer
(American, 1918–1986)
Sam Kramer
(American, 1913–1964)
Silver, turquoise, and garnet
11.4 cm (4 ½ in.)
The Daphne Farago Collection,
2006.288
© Estate of Sam Kramer

37
Pencil bracelet, 1999
Noma Copley
(American, 1916–2006)
Gold, coral, wood, and steel
7.9 cm (3 ⅛ in.)
The Daphne Farago Collection,
2006.108
Reproduced with permission

38
Catherine Deneuve, 1968
Man Ray (Emmanuel Radnitzky,
American, 1890–1976)
Gelatin silver print
10 cm (3 ⅞ in.)
Centre Pompidou, AM
1994-394(5291)
© 2011 Man Ray Trust / Artists
Rights Society (ARS), New York /
ADAGP, Paris
Digital Image © CNAC / MNAM, Dist.
RMN-Grand Palais / Art Resource, NY

39
Pendants Pending, 1970
Man Ray (Emmanuel Radnitzky,
American, 1890–1976)
For GEM Montebello
(Italian, active 1967–78)
Gold
19.1 cm (7 ½ in.)
The Daphne Farago Collection,
2006.465.1-2
© 2015 Man Ray Trust / Artists Rights
Society (ARS), New York / ADAGP,
Paris

40
Earrings, 1940–45
Alexander Calder
(American, 1898–1976)
Silver
15.2 cm (6 in.) each
The Daphne Farago Collection,
2006.88.1-2
© 2025 Calder Foundation, New York /
Artists Rights Society (ARS), New York

41
Lamellae Twisted Cuff, 2016
Zaha Hadid (Iraqi, active in
England, 1950–2016)
For Georg Jensen
(Danish, founded 1904)
Silver
13 cm (5 ⅛ in.)
John H. and Ernestine A.
Payne Fund, 2016.490

42
Lamellae Twisted Cuff for
Georg Jensen by Zaha Hadid
Design, 2016
Christian Högstedt
(Swedish, works in United
States, life dates unknown)
Black and white photograph
Christian Högstedt / Art Partner
Licensing / Trunk Archive

43
Heydar Aliyev Cultural
Centre designed by
Zaha Hadid Architects,
Baku, Azerbaijan, 2013
Iwan Baan (Dutch, born 1975)
Color photograph
Credit: Iwan Baan

44
Necklace, about 1875
Eugène Fontenay
(French, 1823–1887)
Gold
37.9 cm (15 in.)
Museum purchase with funds
donated by the Rita J. and
Stanley H. Kaplan Family
Foundation, 2013.906

45
Necklace, about 1905
Marcus & Co.
(American, 1892–1941)
Gold, platinum, peridot,
diamond, pearl, and enamel
10.2 cm (4 in.)
Gift of Jody Sataloff in memory
of Dr. Joseph Sataloff, 2016.391

46
Sketch for custom pendant,
about 1890–1910
Marcus & Co. (Jaques and
Marcus, American, 1892–1941)
From *Brooches, Pendants* no. 2
Pen and ink with wash on paper
Jewelry Design Books of
Jaques and Marcus, 1890 to
1910, Dartmouth Library, Gift of
Burton Elliott in 1987

47
Seaweed, about 1908
Paul Lienard
(French, 1849–1900)
Gold and pearl
11 cm (4 ⅜ in.)
Gift of Joe and Ruth Sataloff
in honor of Susan B. Kaplan,
2007.892

48
Big Double Gold, 1908
John Paul Cooper
(English, 1869–1933)
Gold, abalone, tourmaline,
moonstone, pearl, amethyst,
and chrysoprase
14 cm (5 ½ in.)
Gift of Susan B. Kaplan,
2008.264

49
Brooch, about 1945
Margret Craver
(American, 1907–2010)
Silver and quartz
4.4 cm (1 ¾ in.)
Gift in memory of Eleanor
Hodge Pough, Wellesley '30,
1991.1050
Reproduced with permission

50
Ring, 1947–48
Margaret De Patta
(American, 1903–1964)
Gold and tourmalinated quartz
3.2 cm (1 ¼ in.)
The Daphne Farago Collection,
2013.1689

51
Ring, about 1955
Claire Falkenstein
(American, 1908–1997)
Silver and glass
6.4 cm (2 ½ in.)
The Daphne Farago Collection,
2006.173
© Falkenstein Foundation, By
Permission.

52
Necklace, about 1959
Betty Cooke
(American, 1924–2024)
Silver
26.7 cm (10 ½ in.)
The Daphne Farago Collection,
2006.102
Copyright © 1959 Betty Cooke

53
Necklace, about 1970–75
Miyé Matsukata
(American, born in Japan,
1922–1981)
Silver, jade, agate, and carnelian
15.2 cm (6 in.)
Gift of Lucy Fields, 1993.893
Reproduced with permission

54
Nana, 1973
Niki de Saint Phalle
(French American, 1930–2002)
Made by Adolfo Del Vivo
(active 20th century)
For GEM Montebello
(Italian, active 1967–78)
Gold and enamel
11.4 cm (4 ½ in.)
The Daphne Farago Collection,
2017.4916
NCAF (Niki Charitable Art Foundation)

55
Girl Blowing Bubbles, about
1910
Fuset y Grau
(Spanish, active 1890s–1930)
Gold, platinum, enamel, pearl,
ivory, sapphire, and diamond
10.2 cm (4 in.)
Museum purchase with funds
donated by Susan B. Kaplan,
William Francis Warden Fund,
Carol Noble in honor of Susan
B. Kaplan, and anonymously,
2012.117

56
Brooch, 1941
Harry Bertoia
(American, born in Italy,
1915–1978)
Silver
13.3 cm (5 ¼ in.)
The Daphne Farago Collection,
2017.4932
© 2025 Estate of Harry Bertoia /
Artists Rights Society (ARS), New York

57
Sun, 1988
Sondra Sherman
(American, born 1958)
Gold-plated bronze
13.3 cm (5 ¼ in.)
The Daphne Farago Collection,
2006.516
© Sondra Sherman

58
The Comedian and the Martyr, 1990
Manfred Bischoff
(German, 1947–2015)
Gold, silver, and coral
10.2 cm (4 in.)
The Daphne Farago Collection, 2006.70

59
Brooch, about 1991
Peter Chang (British, 1944–2017)
Acrylic and metal
14.6 cm (5 ¾ in.)
The Daphne Farago Collection, 2006.95
Reproduced with permission

60
Torque #25D, 1972
Stanley Lechtzin
(American, born 1936)
Silver and resin
19.1 cm (7 ½ in.)
John H. and Ernestine A. Payne Fund and funds donated anonymously in honor of Karen and Michael Rotenberg's 55th anniversary, Karen Rotenberg's birthday, and in memory of Daphne Farago, 2017.4002

61
Blue Breath, 2017
Seulgi Kwon
(Korean, born 1983)
Silicone, pigment, thread, plastic, and feather
17 cm (6 ¾ in.)
Museum purchase with funds donated by Carol Noble in honor of Emily Zilber, 2018.92
Reproduced with Permission by the artist Seulgi Kwon

62
Man and His Pet Bee, 1968
Robert W. Ebendorf
(American, born 1938)
Copper, silver, tintype photograph, glass, brass, aluminum, and other found objects
17.1 cm (6 ¾ in.)
The Daphne Farago Collection, 2006.150

Reproduced with permission

63
Daphne, 2007
Bettina Speckner
(German, born 1962)
Silver, tintype photograph, coral, and maple
9.5 cm (3 ¾ in.)
Museum purchase with funds donated by Joyce Linde in honor of Susan B. Kaplan, 2017.4003
Reproduced with permission

64
Old Lines, 2016
From the series *Oil & Water*, 2015–16
Kat Cole (American, born 1985)
Steel and enamel
18.4 cm (7 ¼ in.)
Gift of Betsy Rowland, 2019.2289

65
Sweet Hearts, 2019
Zachery Lechtenberg
(American, born 1989)
Copper, silver, steel, and enamel
7.6 cm (3 in.)
Anonymous gift, 2021.449

66
Blue Anthurium, 2021
Feng J (Chinese, born 1985)
Gold, Paraiba tourmaline, aquamarine, spinel, sapphire, and diamond
7.5 cm (3 in.)
Gift of the artist, 2023.4
Reproduced with permission

HATHOR-HEADED CRYSTAL PENDANT

67
Hathor-headed crystal pendant (known as the *Head of Hathor*), 743–712 BC
Nubian, Napatan Period, reign of Piankhy (Piye), found in Sudan, el-Kurru, Ku. 55
Gold and rock crystal
5.3 cm (2 in.)
Harvard University—Boston Museum of Fine Arts Expedition, 21.321

CHICLET NECKLACE AND MOSAIC CUFF

68
Chiclet necklace, 1993
Angie Reano Owen (Santo Domingo Pueblo, born 1946)
Turquoise, coral, mother of pearl, lapis lazuli, spiny oyster, and silver
30.5 cm (12 in.)
The Daphne Farago Collection, 2006.406
Reproduced with permission

69
Mosaic cuff, 1995
Angie Reano Owen (Santo Domingo Pueblo, born 1946)
Tiger cowrie, turquoise, spiny oyster, mother-of-pearl, jet, and epoxy
7.3 cm (2 ⅞ in.)
Museum purchase with funds donated by Lois and Stephen Kunian and The Seminarians, 1998.57
Reproduced with permission

FOREVER DANCING— BRIGHT STAR

70
Forever Dancing— Bright Star, 2013
Wallace Chan
(Chinese, born 1956)
Diamond, rock crystal, mother-of-pearl, butterfly specimen, pearl, and titanium
10.6 cm (4 ¼ in.)
Gift of Christin Xing and Rex Wong, 2023.3
Reproduced with permission

JALI

71
Jali, 2024
BHAGAT
(Indian, founded 1877)
Gold, emerald, and diamond
4.3 cm (1 ¾ in.)
William Francis Warden Fund, 2024.2331
© BHAGAT

72
Gateway, about 1677
Indian, Mughal period, found in Delhi area, Northern India
Red sandstone
304.8 cm (120 in.)
Keith McLeod Fund, 1983.386

BODY AS CANVAS

73
Claudette Colbert wearing starfish brooch, 1938
Alfred Eisenstaedt
(German, active in the United States, 1898–1995)
Gelatin silver print
25.4 cm (10 in.)
Frank M. and Mary T. B. Ferrin Fund, 2021.610

74
Starfish brooch, 1937
Juliette Moutard
(French, 1900–1990)
Made by Société Charles Profilet
(French, founded 1927)
For René Boivin
(French, founded 1890)
Gold, ruby, and amethyst
10.8 cm (4 ¼ in.)
Museum purchase with funds donated by the Rita J. and Stanley H. Kaplan Family Foundation, Monica S. Sadler, Otis Norcross Fund, Helen and Alice Colburn Fund, the Curators Circle: Fashion Council, Nancy Adams and Scott Schoen, Seth K. Sweetser Fund, Theresa Baybutt, Emi M. and William G. Winterer, and Deborah Glasser, 2019.654.1

75
Belt with buckle and seven plaques, 8th century
Chinese, Tang Dynasty
Silver and jade
Plaques: 6.2 cm (2 ½ in.)
Buckle: 13.5 cm (5 ⅜ in.)
Marshall H. Gould Fund, 58.692a

76
Fibulae, 19th century
Kabylian (Algeria)
Silver, enamel, and resin
60.5 cm (23 ¾ in.)
Denman Waldo Ross
Collection, 27.405

77
Bodice ornament, 18th century
Probably Spanish
Gold and emerald
22.5 cm (8 ⅞ in.)
Bequest of Mrs. Arthur
Croft—The Gardner Brewer
Collection, 01.6495

78
Corsage ornament, about 1890
Alphonse Auger
(French, 1837–1904)
Silver, gold, and diamond
23 cm (9 in.)
Museum purchase with funds
donated by the Vance Wall
Foundation, Saundra B. Lane
and an anonymous donor,
2012.7

79
Japanesque brooch,
about 1925
Lacloche Frères
(French, 1892–1984)
Platinum, gold, enamel,
diamond, ruby, and onyx
5.2 cm (2 in.)
William Francis Warden Fund,
2009.2533

80
Queen Mary, about 1920
Hay Wrightson
(English, 1874–1949)
Published by Raphael Tuck &
Sons (English, 1886–1960)
Photograph on cardstock
14 cm (5 ½ in.)
Leonard A. Lauder Postcard
Archive—Gift of Leonard A.
Lauder, 2015.7552

81
Flore, 1925
Lucien Lelong
(French, 1889–1958)
Gouache on paper
25.4 cm (10 in.)
Gift of Jean S. and Frederic A.
Sharf, 2013.2064

82–83
Duette, 1944
Adolph Katz
(active 20th century)
For Coro (American, 1901–1979)
Gold-plated silver, glass,
and enamel
4.8 cm (1 ⅞ in.) each
Gift of Carole Tanenbaum,
2018.3911

84
Maltese cross brooch, 1970s
Maison Gripoix
(French, founded 1890)
For House of Chanel
(French, founded 1909)
Metal and glass
7.1 cm (2 ⅞ in.)
Museum purchase with funds
donated by Penny Vinik,
2008.34

85
Coco Chanel, Paris, about 1937
Horst P. Horst (American,
born in Germany, 1906–1999)
Gelatin silver print
28.4 cm (11 ¼ in.)
The Howard Greenberg
Collection—Museum purchase
with funds donated by the
Phillip Leonian and Edith
Rosenbaum Leonian Charitable
Trust, 2018.3396
© Conde Nast

86
Bow necklace, 1983
House of Chanel
(French, founded 1909)
Metal and glass
46.5 cm (18 ⅜ in.)
William E. Nickerson Fund
and funds donated by Marc S.
Plonskier, 2019.537

87
Lily of the Valley, 1950s
Probably Maison Gripoix
(French, founded 1890)
For House of Christian Dior
(French, founded 1946)
Metal and glass
61 cm (24 in.)
William E. Nickerson Fund
and funds donated by Marc S.
Plonskier, 2019.541

88
You, 2013
Elie Top (Flemish, active in
France, born 1976)
For House of Lanvin
(French, founded 1890)
Metal, resin, glass, and silk
10.5 cm (4 ⅛ in.)
Gift of Carole Tanenbaum,
2018.4014

89
Model wearing Art Smith's
Modern Cuff, about 1948
Peter Basch
(American, 1921–2004)
Gelatin silver print
Photo © Estate of Peter Basch,
courtesy of Estate of Peter Basch

90
Model wearing Pierre Cardin
design, 1969
Otto Bettmann
(German American, 1903–1998)
Black and white photograph
Bettmann via Getty Images

91
Pierre Cardin
(French, 1922–2020)
Necklace, 1971
Chrome and acrylic
36 cm (14 ¼ in.)
Gift of Karen and Michael
Rotenberg, 2010.304
Reproduced with permission

92
Liza Minnelli wearing
Large Bone Cuff by Elsa
Peretti for Tiffany & Co., 1972
Jack Mitchell
(American, 1925-2013)
Black and white photograph
Jack Mitchell / Archive Photos via
Getty Images

93
Large Bone Cuff, about 1978
Elsa Peretti
(Italian, 1940–2021)
For Tiffany & Co.
(American, founded 1837)
Silver
11.4 cm (4 ½ in.)
Gift of Monica S. Sadler in
honor of Katy Kane, 2018.3218
© Nando and Elsa Peretti Foundation

94
Python Hot Pants, 2016
Mallory Weston
(American, born 1986)
Gold-filled bronze, silver, copper,
steel, leather, and cotton
40.6 cm (16 in.)
Museum purchase with funds
donated by Carol Shasha
Green, 2022.96

95
Tiara-necklace, about 1912
Probably Boucheron
(French, founded 1858)
Platinum and diamond
17 cm (6 ¾ in.)
Gift of the heirs of Bettina
Looram de Rothschild,
2013.1775

96
Raven's Tail, 2017–18
Evelyn Vanderhoop
(Haida, born 1953)
Wool, sea otter fur, cedar bark
fiber, shell, and copper thread
152.4 cm (60 in.)
William Francis Warden Fund,
Heritage Fund for a Diverse
Collection, and Gallery
Instructor 50th Anniversary
Fund to support The Heritage
Fund for a Diverse Collection,
2017.4182
© Evelyn Vanderhoop
Photograph by Bernadette Jarrard

97
Naaxiin Ghost Face, 2022
Tiffany Vanderhoop
(Aquinnah Wampanoag and
Haida, born 1982)
Brass and glass
17.8 cm (7 in.)
Textile Curator's Fund,
2023.437.1
Reproduced with permission

98
Sea Creatures, 2015
Mariko Kusumoto
(Japanese, born 1967)
Polyester organza and
monofilament
31.1 cm (12 ¼ in.)
Gift of Mobilia Gallery in
memory of the artist's father,
2016.87
Reproduced with permission

99
Model Soo Joo Park wears the
Big in Japan ensemble while
walking for Jean-Paul Gaultier
at Paris Fashion Week, 2019
Pascal Le Segretain
(French, born 1964)
Color photograph
Getty Images Entertainment via Getty
Images

100
Renaissance Revival neck
ornament, 1900–1904
G. Paulding Farnham
(American, 1859–1927)
For Tiffany & Co.
(American, founded 1837)
Platinum, gold, enamel, diamond,
ruby, emerald, cat's eye,
chrysoberyl, sapphire, and pearl
147.3 cm (58 in.)
Gift of Susan B. Kaplan,
2015.3184

101
Françoise de Longwy,
about 1527
Circle of Corneille de Lyon
(French, active by 1533,
died 1575)
Oil on panel
14.6 cm (5 ¾ in.)
Bartlett Collection—Museum
purchase with funds from
the Francis Bartlett Donation
of 1912, 19.764

102
Necklace, 1920s
Miao (China)
Silver
29.2 cm (11 ½ in.)
Gift of Jacqueline Loewe
Fowler, 2010.1371

103
Necklace, about 1986
Bulgari
(Italian, founded 1884)
Gold, pearl, tourmaline, citrine,
and peridot
16.5 cm (6 ½ in.)
Gift of Bulgari, 2010.597
Bulgari SPA, Heritage
Department, Rome

104
Ear rods, 700–1520
Coclé (Panama)
Gold and greenstone
8.3 cm (3 ¼ in.) and 10 cm (4 in.)
Museum purchase with funds
donated by Landon T. Clay,
1971.926-8

105
Drinking vessel, 650–850
Mayan, Late Classic Period,
found in El Petén, Guatemala
Earthenware with slip paint
19.4 cm (7 ⅝ in.)
Museum purchase with funds
donated by Lavinia and Landon
T. Clay, 2007.423

106
Marsh-bird brooch, 1901–2
Charles Robert Ashbee
(English, 1863–1942)
Made by Adolf Gebhardt
(active in England, early
19th century)
Enamel by William Mark
(Australian, active in England,
1868–1956)
Gold, silver, enamel,
moonstone, topaz, and pearl
10.5 cm (4 ⅛ in.)
Museum purchase with funds
donated by Susan B. Kaplan,
Marshall H. Gould Fund, John
H. and Ernestine A. Payne
Fund, Linda Fenton, Dorothy-
Lee Jones Fund, Penny Vinik,
and Adrienne Iselin Gilbert
Memorial Fund, 2007.827

107
Branching, 1967
merry renk
(American, 1921–2012)
Silver and pearl
18.4 cm (7 ¼ in.)
Gift of Joan Pearson Watkins
in honor of C. Malcolm
Watkins, 1986.912
© renk

108
Secret, interrupted, 1998
Ann Ray
(French, born 1969)
Gelatin silver print
40.6 cm (16 in.)
Gift of the artist in memory
of Lee Alexander McQueen,
2021.1013

109
*Paula Gellibrand, Marquise de
Casa Maury*, 1928
Cecil Beaton
(English, 1904–1980)
Gelatin silver print
45.7 cm (18 in.)
Abbott Lawrence Fund,
2006.1371
© Cecil Beaton Archive / Condé Nast

110
Pomander, about 1580
English
Gilded silver
6.4 cm (2 ½ in.)
Bequest of Frank Brewer
Bemis, 35.1547

111
Portrait of a Woman, 1581
Frans Pourbus the Elder
(Netherlandish, 1545–1581)
Oil on panel
142.9 cm (56 ¼ in.)
William Sturgis Bigelow
Collection, 27.176

112
*China: a Manchu lady having
her face painted, Beijing*, 1869
John Thomson
(Scottish, 1837–1921)
Glass plate negative
Wellcome Collection, 19668i

113
Hairpin, 19th century
Chinese
Metal, kingfisher feather,
jade, coral, colored gemstones,
imitation pearl, and silk-
wrapped wire
10.5 cm (4 ⅛ in.)
William Sturgis Bigelow
Collection, RES.11.4514

114
Enchanted Ania, 2023
Anna Hu
(Taiwanese, active in the
United States, born 1977)
Titanium, spinel, and diamond
19.3 cm (7 ⅝ in.)
Gift of Dr. Christina S. Yao,
2024.2242
© Anna Hu Haute Joaillerie

ROTHSCHILD BROOCH
AND NECKLACE-TIARA

115
Baron and Baroness Alphonse
and Clarice de Rothschild with
their children, Albert, Bettina,
and Gwendoline, 1937
Probably gelatin silver print
Courtesy of Bettina Burr

116
Art Deco brooch, about 1937
Josef Siess Söhne
(Austrian, 1867–1922)
Platinum, gold, emerald,
and diamond
1.9 cm (¾ in.)
Gift of the heirs of Bettina
Looram de Rothschild,
2013.1777

117
Necklace-tiara, about 1880
European
Silver, gold, pearl, and diamond
18.5 cm (7 ⅜ in.)
Gift of the heirs of Bettina
Looram de Rothschild,
2013.1774.1

118
Clarice de Rothschild, 1925
Philip de László
(Hungarian, 1869–1937)
Oil on canvas
109.2 cm (43 in.)
Gift of the heirs of Bettina
Looram de Rothschild, 2015.110

GOLDFINGER

119
Goldfinger, 1969
Bruno Martinazzi
(Italian, 1923–2018)
Gold
7.3 cm (2 ⅞ in.)
The Daphne Farago Collection,
2006.346
© Bruno Martinazzi

WE TWO

120
Joyce J. Scott wearing *We
Two*, about 1993–96
John Dean
(American, born 1955)
Black and white photograph
Reproduced with permission

121
We *Two,* after 1974
Joyce J. Scott (American, born
1948); Art Smith (American,
born in Cuba, 1917–1982)
Brass, glass, and leather
20.3 cm (8 in.)
Gallery Instructor 50th
Anniversary Fund to support
of the Heritage Fund for
a Diverse Collection and
funds donated by Stephen
Borkowski, 2016.82
Reproduced with permission

STATEMENT JEWELS

122
Woman smoking on a bicycle
From the series *All Heil*, 1900
Raphael Kirchner
(Austrian, 1875–1917)
Lithograph on cardstock
14 cm (5 ½ in.)
Leonard A. Lauder Postcard
Archive—Gift of Leonard A.
Lauder, 2012.6092.8

123
Bicycle brooch, mid-1890s
Attributed to Streeter & Co.,
LTD (English, about 1867–1905)
Gold, enamel, diamond,
and ruby
6.5 cm (2 ⅝ in.)
Museum purchase with
funds donated anonymously,
2009.2419

124
*Am I Not a Man and a
Brother?*, 1786–87
Wedgwood Manufactory
(English, founded 1759)
Jasperware and gold
3 cm (1 ¼ in.)
Bequest of Mrs. Richard Baker,
96.779

125
Flag brooch, 1917
Probably Oscar Heyman Bros.
(American, founded 1912)
For Black, Starr and Frost
(American, 1876–1929)
Platinum, diamond, ruby,
and sapphire
6.4 cm (2 ½ in.)
Gift of Selina F. Little in
memory of Nina Fletcher Little,
2004.2080

126
Emblem of the Americas, 1941
Lester Gaba
(American, 1907–1987)
For Coro
(American, 1901–1979)
Gold-plated metal and epoxy
6.6 cm (2 ½ in.)
Gift of Carole Tanenbaum,
2018.4039

127
Nelson Mandela (1918–2013)
wearing traditional beads
during his time in hiding from
the police, South Africa, 1961
Eli Weinberg
(Latvian, worked in South
Africa, 1908–1981)
Black and white photograph
Eli Weinberg / Universal History
Archive / Universal Images Group via
Getty Images

128
Portrait of Secretary Albright,
as reproduced on the cover
of Helen W. Drutt English's
1998 book *Brooching It
Diplomatically: A Tribute to
Madeleine K. Albright*, 2005
Timothy Greenfield-Sanders
(American, born 1952)
Color photograph
Portrait by © Timothy Greenfield-
Sanders

129
Beaded collar, early 20th century
Xhosa
(Ciskei, South Africa)
Glass, shell, and sinew
31.1 cm (12 ¼ in.)
Gift of Drs. James and Gladys
Strain and Dr. Jamie P. Strain,
2005.1203

130
Bracelet with image of Hathor,
250–100 BC
Nubian, Meroitic Period,
found in Sudan, Gebel Barkal,
Pyramid 8
Gold and enamel
5.7 cm (2 ¼ in.)
Harvard University—Boston
Museum of Fine Arts
Expedition, 20.333

131
Pendant depicting the ten
incarnations of Vishnu, early
18th century
Indian (Jaipur, Rajasthan)
Gold, sapphire, diamond,
emerald, ruby, and enamel
4.9 cm (2 in.)
Otis Norcross Fund, 39.764

132
Jewish wedding ring,
19th century
Central European
Gold and enamel
1.9 cm (¾ in.)
Anonymous Centennial gift,
69.1096

133
Jewish engagement or wedding
ring, early 14th century
German, found in Weissenfels
Gold-plated silver
3.2 cm (1 ¼ in.)
Sachsen-Anhalt Cultural
Foundation - Moritzburg Art
Museum, Halle (Saale)
Photo: PUNCTUM / B. Kober

134
Mourning pendant-brooch, 1792
Rowland Parry (American,
active about 1790–96)
Case by James Musgrave
(American, active 1792–
about 1813)
Hairwork by Jeremiah Boone
(American, active about
1790–96)
Gold, watercolor on ivory, hair,
and glass
5.7 cm (2¼ in.)
The Daphne Farago Collection,
2006.418

135
Brooch with matching earrings,
about 1860
Gold, enamel, and diamond
Brooch: 3 cm (1¼ in.)
Earrings: 2.4 cm (1 in.) each
Museum purchase with funds
donated by Susan B. Kaplan and
by exchange from a Bequest
of Maxim Karolik, The Elizabeth
Day McCormick Collection,
Gift of Mrs. Willian Reynolds, Gift
of Mrs. Alfred Redfield, Gift of
Mrs. Samuel Cabot, Gift of Mrs.
Oric Bates, Gift of Miss Eleanor
Randall, Gift of Miss Eleanor E.
Barry, Gift of Mrs. Lorenz E.
Ernst, Gift of Miss Penelope B.
Noyes from the Estate of Mrs.
Winthrop H. Wade, Gift of Mrs.
Charles H. Pease, Gift from the
Estate of Mary Babcock Alward,
Gift of Mrs. George E. Bates,
Gift of Miss Helen R. Humpage
in memory of William and
Winifred Humpage, and Gift in
memory of Mary Wade White
from her children, 2008.313,
2008.314.1-2

136
Pages from *Frank Leslie's
Illustrated Newspaper*
advertising sale of Mary Todd
Lincoln's wardrobe and jewelry
From *Frank Leslie's Illustrated
Newspaper*, October 10, 1867
Ink on paper

137
Bracelet, 1864
North American or European
Gold, glass, and hair
9.5 cm (3¾ in.)
Gift of Mrs. Joseph A.
Cushman, 64.735

138
*Grace Charlotte Rose
(née Snow), Lady Rose*, 1866
Frederick Sandys
(English, 1829–1904)
Oil on panel
55.9 cm (22 in.)
Yale Center for British Art,
Paul Mellon Fund, B1993.20

139
Enuh (Life), 2008
Lyndon Tsosie
(Diné [Navajo], born 1968)
Silver, gold, sugilite, lapis lazuli,
spiny oyster, and boulder opal
12.7 cm (5 in.)
Gift of Vicki Howard, 2019.2285

140
*The Marriage of Queen
Victoria, 10 February 1840*,
1840–42
Sir George Hayter
(British, 1792–1871)
Oil on canvas
273.5 cm (107⅝ in.)
The Royal Collection Trust,
RCIN 407165

141
Coburg Eagle brooch, 1840
Prince Consort Albert
(English, 1819–1861)
Made by Charles Augustus du
Vé (British, active in 1840)
Gold, turquoise, pearl, ruby,
and diamond
4.5 cm (1¾ in.)
Museum purchase with funds
donated by the Rita J. and
Stanley H. Kaplan Family
Foundation, 2020.146

142
Pompadour at Her Toilette,
1750, with later additions
François Boucher
(French, 1703–1770)
Oil on canvas
81.2 cm (32 in.)
Harvard Art Museums / Fogg
Museum, Bequest of Charles E.
Dunlap, 1966.47

143
Necklace with a cameo of
Elizabeth I, about 1890
Mrs. Philip (Charlotte)
Newman (English, 1840–1927)
Carved by Georges Bissinger
(German, active in Paris, late
19th century)
Gold, silver, diamond, emerald,
pearl, agate, and glass
3.8 cm (1½ in.)
Museum purchase with funds
donated by Susan B. Kaplan,
2011.7

144 145
Shaving (*Viewfinder*), 2017
Melanie Bilenker
(American, born 1978)
Hair on paper, mineral crystal,
mother-of-pearl, gold, and
silver
6.4 cm (2½ in.)
Museum purchase with funds
donated by Carol Shasha
Green, 2021.663

146
Scorpion, 1978
Elsa Peretti
(Italian, 1940–2021)
For Tiffany & Co.
(American, founded 1837)
Silver
33 cm (13 in.)
Gift of Monica S. Sadler,
2017.4179

147
Colt family necklace and
earrings, 1856
Tiffany & Co.
(American, founded 1837)
Gold, enamel, and diamond
15.5 cm (6⅛ in.)
Frank B. Bemis Fund, William
Francis Warden Fund, and
funds donated anonymously,
2010.221.1

148
Pectoral shell necklace,
20th century
Papua New Guinean,
acquired in Indonesia
Kina shell and plant fiber
19 cm (7½ in.)
Gift of the McMillan-Stewart
Foundation, 2013.33

149
Necklace, 12th century
Eastern Javanese, found in
Central Java, Indonesia
Gold
19 cm (7½ in.)
Frederick L. Jack Fund, 1981.44

150
Hair pendants, 19th–early
20th century
Lhasa Tibetan
Turquoise and silver
14.5 cm (5¾ in.) each
The Elizabeth Day McCormick
Collection, 46.1442a–b

151
Armorial bracelet, about 1830
Simon Petiteau
(French, born 1782)
Gold, pearl, emerald, ruby,
and diamond
16.5 cm (6½ in.)
Museum purchase with funds
donated by the David and
Roberta Logie Department of
Textile and Fashion Arts
Visiting Committee in honor of
Yvonne J. Markowitz, Rita J.
Kaplan and Susan B. Kaplan
Curator Emerita of Jewelry,
2014.1866

Iris Bodemer (German, born 1970); Kristine Bolhuis (American, born 1971); Helen Britton (Australian, born 1966); Lola Brooks (American, born 1970); Doug Bucci (American, born 1970); Raïssa Bump (American, born 1980); David Chatt (American, born 1960); Sharon Church (American, born 1948); Liz Clark (American, born 1982); Emily Cobb (American, born 1987); Nikki Couppee (American, born 1983); Erin Shay Daily (American, born 1975); Venetia Dale (American, born 1981); Noam Elyashiv (Israeli, active in the United States, born 1963); Sandra Enterline (American, born 1960); Pat Flynn (American, born 1954); Warwick Freeman (born in New Zealand in 1953); Donald Friedlich (American, born 1954); Susie Ganch (American, born 1971); Caroline Gore (American, born 1976); Adam Grinovich (American, born 1981); Heather Guidero (American, born 1980); Gésine Hackenberg (German, born 1972); Mielle Harvey (American, born 1971); Arthur Hash (American, born 1976); Lauren Kalman (American, born 1980); Dahlia Kanner (American, born 1974); John Kennedy (American, born 1954); Janis Kerman (Canadian, born 1957); Gabriella Kiss (American, born 1959); Anya Kivarkis (American, born 1975); Esther Knobel (Israeli, born in Poland in 1949); Monika Krol (American, born 1984); Daniel Kruger (South African, works in Germany, born 1951); Julia Maria Künnap (Estonian, born 1979); Akiko Kurihara (Japanese, works in Italy, born 1975); Jacqueline Lillie (Austrian, born in France in 1941); Märta Mattsson

(Swedish, born 1982); Paul McClure (Canadian, born 1967); Bruce Metcalf (American, born 1949); Myra Mimlitch-Gray (American, born 1962); Darcy Miro (American, born 1973); Emiko Oye (American, born 1974); Seth Papac (American, born 1981); Tom Patti (American, born 1943); Mary Hallam Pearse (American, born 1969); Maria Phillips (American, born 1963); Suzanne Pugh (American, born 1972); Leonardo Quiles (American, born 1971); Tina Rath (American, born 1968); Ruta Reifen (Israeli, works in Israel and the United States, born 1984); Lucy Sarneel (Dutch, 1961–2020); Biba Schutz (American, born 1946); Barbara Seidenath (German, active in the United States, born 1960); Sondra Sherman (American, born 1958); Carina Shoshtary (German, born 1979); Bettina Speckner (German, born 1962); Tracy Steepy (American, born 1973); Lori Talcott (American, born 1959); Amy Tavern (American, born 1974); Lauren Tickle (American, born 1985); Julia Turner (American, born 1970); Johan van Aswegen (American, born in South Africa in 1958); Manon van Kouswijk (Dutch, works in Australia, born 1967); Jonathan Wahl (American, born 1968); Stacey Lee Webber (American, born 1982); Brian Weissman (American, born 1976); Mallory Weston (American, born 1986); Deb Todd Wheeler (American, born 1965); Petra Zimmermann (Austrian, born 1975)
Sterling silver
Bracelet: 35.6 cm (14 in.)
Charms: 2.5 cm (1 in.) each, 79 total
Gift of Sienna Patti, 2019.806.1-80
© Sienna Patti

171
Beadnet dress, 2551–2528 BC
Egyptian, Old Kingdom, Dynasty 4, reign of Khufu, found in Tomb G 7440 Z, Giza
Faience
113 cm (44 ½ in.)
Harvard University—Boston Museum of Fine Arts Expedition, 27.1548.1

172
Jewelry found at pyramids of Kashta, Piye, Shebitku, and Tanutamani, in El Kurru, Nubia (present-day Sudan), 1919
Glass plate negative
Harvard University—Boston Museum of Fine Arts Expedition, A2775A_NS

173
Amulet box, 19th century
Iranian
Turquoise, glass, silver, and silk
5 cm (2 in.)
Bequest of Mrs. Arthur Croft—The Gardner Brewer Collection, 01.6508

174
Medallion, 2022
Elizabeth James-Perry (Aquinnah Wampanoag, born 1973)
Wampum and walnut-dyed deerskin
61 cm (24 in.)
H. E. Bolles Fund and The Heritage Fund for a Diverse Collection, 2022.12
© Elizabeth James-Perry

175
Muhammad Shah in a garden, about 1730–40
Probably Chitarman (Indian, active about 1715–60)
Indian, Mughal period
Ink on paper
43.4 cm (17 ⅛ in.)
Arthur Mason Knapp Fund, 26.283

176
Cast iron brooch, before 1849
German
Iron
9 cm (3 ½ in.)
Gift of Miss Alice M. Longfellow and Mrs. Joseph G. Thorp, 17.203

177
Dahlia dye press, part one of two, 1957–64
Louis Féron Inc. (American, 1958–2004)
Brass and zinc
7.6 cm (3 in.)

178
Dahlia Compact, 1959
Jean Schlumberger (French, active in the United States, 1907–1987)
Made by Louis Féron Inc. (American, 1958–2004)
For Tiffany & Co. (American, founded 1837)
Gold and sapphire
7 cm (2 ¾ in.)
Museum purchase with funds donated by the Rita J. and Stanley H. Kaplan Family Foundation and Jean S. and Frederic A. Sharf, 2015.150.1-3

179
Big Pimpin', 2014
Tanya Crane (American, born 1974)
Gold-plated brass, gold, copper, enamel, and gold leaf
61 cm (24 in.)
The Heritage Fund for a Diverse Collection, 2021.448

180
Detail of fig. 159

181
Wedding ring, 1773
Paul Revere, Jr. (American, 1734–1818)
Gold
1 cm (⅜ in.)
Gift of Mrs. Henry B. Chapin and Edward H. R. Revere, 56.585

ACKNOWLEDGMENTS

The MFA's jewelry collection spans nearly all of the institution's curatorial departments, and this catalogue was a similarly collaborative endeavor. Beyond Museum walls, *Brilliance* benefited from the knowledge of colleagues, scholarship new and old, and the partnership of artists and collectors from around the globe.

My thanks go to Pierre Terjanian, Ann and Graham Gund Director; and Matthew Teitelbaum, Ann and Graham Gund Director Emeritus, for their support; as well as to Susan B. Kaplan; Rebecca Tobin, Executive Director of the Rita J. and Stanley H. Kaplan Family Foundation; and the Foundation's trustees. This book marries the interests of the Kaplans, who founded a business in the field of education and for whom jewelry was always a creative pursuit. The text would not be as beautifully organized or as well written without the direction of editor Claire Pask, nor would it have been as beautifully designed or illustrated without the work of Beverly Joel and MFA staff photographers, especially Michael Gould.

In the David and Roberta Logie Department of Fashion, Textiles, and Jewelry, I was guided by the support of Elizabeth Dospěl Williams, Penny Vinik Chair of Fashion, Textiles, and Jewelry; Jennifer Swope, David and Roberta Logie Curator of Textiles; theo tyson; Carly Bieterman; and Lauren Whitlock. For three years, Tzu-Ju Chen provided research support for jewelry projects, including *Brilliance*, that resulted in exciting new information on the objects in the MFA's collection. I am honored to have been mentored by Yvonne Markowitz, Rita J. Kaplan and Susan B. Kaplan Curator of Jewelry Emerita, whose work is pivotal to my thinking.

The objects on these pages look their best because of the masterful work of Mei-an Tsu and Emilie Tréhu in the MFA's Objects Conservation Lab and the partnership of Sarah Tuner, Tracey Jenkins Darji, and Haley Filamond at the North Bennett Street School.

The support of Emily Blumenthal, Chief of Staff; and Christina Yu Yu, Matsutaro Shoriki Chair, Art of Asia, was essential to the success of this catalogue. The expertise of my curatorial colleagues at the Museum left an important mark on this publication. This book is the result of over a decade of study. My scholarship has been refined through conversations with colleagues near and far: Theresa Baybutt, Ariana Bishop, Claudine Seroussi Bretagne, Claire de Truchis-Lauriston and the Boucheron archives team, Emefa Cole, Tefkros Iordanis Sophocleous Christou, Vanessa Cron, Susan Cummins, Sarah Davis, Ulysses Dietz, Inezita Gay Eckel, Richard Edgecomb, Elyse Karlin, Neil Lane, Suzanne van Leeuwen, Pierce MacGuire, Catharina Manchanda, Helen Molesworth, Geoffrey Munn, Lucinda Orr, Jane Perry, Claire Phillips, Katherine Purcell, Anna Tabakhova, Cristina Vignone and the staff at Tiffany & Co. archives, Jaci Rohr, Juliette de Rouchefault, Mathieu Rousset-Perrier, Raquel Alonso Perez, Sheila Smithie, Beth Wees, Joanna Whalley, Cecilia Wichmann, Diane Wright, Christopher Young, and Janet Zapata. I am grateful to Janis Staggs at Neue Galerie New York, and, in Paris, to Florent Guérif, Léa Krief, Laurence Mouillefarine, Evelyne Possémé, and Sebastien Quequet. Finally, I am humbled by the generosity of the many donors who have given jewelry to the MFA, thus making a project like this possible.

Art museums are nothing without artists. I am honored by the trust and kindness of so many creatives, past and present. *Brilliance* is immeasurably strengthened by the perspectives of nine such contributors. To Bettina Burr, Tanya Crane, Helen Drutt English, Melanie Grant, Yasmin Hemmerle, Amin Jaffer, Henrietta Lidchi, Bella Neyman, Victoria Reed, Kendall Reiss, and Joyce J. Scott—thank you!

This book is dedicated to my family: Cody, Grace, and Mark Stoehrer.

Emily Stoehrer
Rita J. Kaplan and Susan B. Kaplan Senior Curator of Jewelry at
the Museum of Fine Arts, Boston

CONTRIBUTORS

EMILY STOEHRER is Rita J. Kaplan and Susan B. Kaplan Senior Curator of Jewelry at the Museum of Fine Arts, Boston.

BETTINA BURR is an Honorary Trustee at the Museum of Fine Arts, Boston.

TANYA CRANE is an artist, 2024 United States Artist Fellow in Craft, and Assistant Professor of 3D Foundations, Jewelry, and Sculpture at Long Beach City College.

HELEN W. DRUTT ENGLISH is a curator, craft historian, author, educator, and former gallerist.

MELANIE GRANT is an author, curator, and Executive Consultant for the Responsible Jewellery Council.

YASMIN HEMMERLE, alongside her husband Christian Hemmerle, is at the helm of the German, fourth-generation, family-run jewelry house Hemmerle.

AMIN JAFFER is Director of The Al Thani Collection.

HENRIETTA LIDCHI is a researcher and curator, and currently Executive Director of the Wheelwright Museum of the American Indian.

BELLA NEYMAN is an independent curator, author, lecturer, and co-founder of NYC Jewelry Week.

VICTORIA REED is Bettina Burr Chair of Provenance at the Museum of Fine Arts, Boston.

KENDALL REISS is an artist and gallerist, as well as Professor of the Practice in Metals and Chair of 3D and Performance at the School of the Museum of Fine Arts at Tufts University.

JOYCE J. SCOTT is a multimedia artist and 2016 Fellow of the John D. and Catherine T. MacArthur Foundation.

INDEX

MFÆBoston

MFA Publications
Museum of Fine Arts, Boston
465 Huntington Avenue
Boston, Massachusetts 02115
mfa.org/publications

Generous support for this publication is provided by the Andrew W. Mellon Publications Fund. Additional support is provided by the MFA Associates / Senior Associates Tribute Fund in Memory of Past Members and the Ann and John Clarkeson Lecture and Publication Fund for Textiles and Costumes.

ISBN 978-0-87846-905-5
LCCN 2025938607

The Museum of Fine Arts, Boston, is a nonprofit institution devoted to the promotion and appreciation of the creative arts. The Museum endeavors to respect the copyrights of all authors and creators in a manner consistent with its nonprofit educational mission. If you feel any material has been included in this publication improperly, please contact the Department of Intellectual Property at 617 267 9300, or by mail at the above address.

While the objects in this publication necessarily represent only a small portion of the MFA's holdings, information about approximately 400,000 objects is available to the public worldwide. To learn more about the MFA's collections, including provenance, publication, and exhibition history, kindly visit mfa.org/collections.

For a complete listing of MFA publications, please contact the publisher at the above address, or call 617 369 4233.

Front cover: Eugène Fontenay, necklace, about 1875 (detail, fig. 44)

Back cover: Wallace Chan, *Forever Dancing—Bright Star*, 2013 (detail, fig. 70)

Details by page: p. 2–3: Joyce J. Scott and Art Smith, *We Two*, after 1974 (detail, fig. 121); p. 12–13: Mary Lee Hu, *Choker #88*, 2005 (detail, fig. 10); p. 25: Charlene Sanchez Reano and Frank Reano, *Thunderbird*, 2009 (detail, fig. 21); p. 89: Bulgari, necklace, about 1986 (detail, fig. 103); p. 138–39: Anton Frühauf, *King's Bracelet*, 1959 (detail, fig. 152)

Illustrations in this book were photographed by Imaging Studios, Museum of Fine Arts, Boston, except where otherwise noted.

Edited by Claire Pask
Proofread by Fronia W. Simpson
Indexed by Shannon Li
Principal photography by Michael Gould
Design and production by pulp, ink.

Typeset in Calibre and Louize
Printed on Condat matt Périgord
Printed and bound at Brizzolis

Distributed by
ARTBOOK | D.A.P.
75 Broad Street, Suite 630
New York, New York 10004
artbook.com

First edition
Printed and bound in Spain
This book was printed on acid-free paper.